The Auxilia of the Roman Imperial Army
By George Cheesman

(1914)

CW01081491

PREFACE

The following essay is an attempt to deal with an interesting branch of Roman military history which has not previously been made the subject of an independent treatise. In a study of this kind, which relies largely upon epigraphical evidence to which additions are constantly being made, it is equally necessary that the scattered material available should at intervals be collected and utilized, and that the unfortunate collector should realize that his conclusions will inevitably be revised in the future in the light of fresh evidence. I hope, accordingly, that I have made some use of all sources of information available without acquiring or expressing excessive confidence in the finality of my deductions. Students of the military system of the Roman Empire may complain that a certain number of complicated questions are too summarily disposed of in the following pages, but if discussion of the evidence in detail has been occasionally omitted with the idea of keeping the size of this book within reasonable limits, I hope that I have been careful to indicate where uncertainty lies.

I have in many places been glad to acknowledge my indebtedness to my predecessors in this field of study, who in one branch of the subject or another have removed so many difficulties from my path. To two scholars, however, my debt is too extensive and general to have received adequate recognition in the footnotes. Mommsen's article, ' Die Conscriptionsordnung der römischen Kaiserzeit,' was written thirty years ago ; I have, I hope, been diligent in collecting the evidence which has since accumulated, but I have found little to induce me to leave the path indicated by the founder of the scientific study of the Roman Empire. I owe much to Professor A. von Domaszewski's ingenious and comprehensive work, *Die Rangordnung des römischen Heeres,* and feel my obligation to its learning and suggestiveness none the less that I have sometimes been compelled to differ from the conclusions stated in it. I am also deeply indebted to Professor Haverfield for constant encouragement and much valuable criticism, and can only wish that this essay were a more adequate testimony to the value of his influence upon the study of Roman history at Oxford. I desire also to express my gratitude to my colleague, Mr. N. Whatley, of Hertford College, for reading this essay in manuscript, and making many valuable suggestions.

G. L. CHEESMAN.

New College, Oxford. *(1914)*

LIST OF ABBREVIATIONS EMPLOYED

The *Corpus Inscriptionum Latinarum* is referred to simply by the numbers of the volumes without any prefix.
The military diplomata (D) are referred to by the revised numbering given in the supplement to the third volume of the *Corpus.*
Eph..Ep. = *Ephemeris Epigraphica.*
A. E. = *L'année épigraphique,* edited by MM. Cagnat and Besnier.
I. G. R. R. = *Inscriptiones Graecae ad res Romanas pertinentes,* edited by Cagnat.

A. J. B. = *Bonner Jahrbücher*, the periodical of the *Verein von Altertumsfreunden im Rheinlande*.
W. D. Z. = *Westdeutsche Zeitschrift*.
B. G. U. = *Ägyptische Urkunden aus den königlichen Museen zu Berlin*.
Mommsen *Conscriptionsordnung* = Mommsen, *Die Conscriptions-ordnung der römischen Kaiserzeit*, published in volume vi of the *Gesammelte Schriften*.
von Dom. *Rangordnung* = A. von Domaszewski, *Die Rangord-nung des römischen Heeres*, Bonn, 1907.
von Dom. *Sold* = A. von Domaszewski, *Der Truppensold der Kaiserzeit*, in volume χ of the *Neue Heidelberger Jahrbücher*.
J. R. S. = *The Journal of Roman Studies*.

INTRODUCTION.THE MILITARY REFORMS OF AUGUSTUS

An essay on the Roman auxilia might seem merely to be one of the many monographs in which students of the military system of the Roman Empire are patiently arranging material for some future scholar to utilize in a more comprehensive work. But while much space must necessarily be devoted to details of military organization, the subject opens up social and political questions of wider range. The extent to which a ruling race can safely use the military resources of its subjects and the effect on both parties of such a relation, the advantages and dangers of a defensive or an aggressive frontier policy, these are questions of universal historical interest, on which even an essay of so limited a scope as this must necessarily touch in passing.

As a preliminary consideration it must be realized that the use of troops drawn from the subject races was not an invention of the imperial government, but goes back to the most flourishing days of the Republic. The heavy-armed yet mobile infantry which formed the greater part of the burgess militia of the *cives Romani* and the *socii* constituted an arm which won for Rome the hegemony of Italy, and triumphed alike over the numbers and courage of Ligurian and Gaul or the disciplined professional armies of Carthage and the Hellenistic monarchies. In other branches of the service, however, the republican armies were less superior. Their cavalry, drawn, as was usual in the citizen armies of the ancient world, from the wealthier classes, was not sufficiently numerous and proved no match for its opponents in the Second Punic War. The light troops came off even worse when engaged either with mountain tribes fighting on their own ground or with the skilled archers and slingers of Carthage or Macedon. So early was this recognized that, in describing an offer made by Hiero of Syracuse to furnish a thousand archers and slingers in 217 b.c., Livy is able to make the Syracusans justify the suggestion to Roman pride by asserting that it was already customary for the Republic to use *externi* in this capacity. To make up their notorious deficiency in this respect the Government could have recourse to three sources of supply. They could, as in this case, accept or demand contingents from allies outside the Italian military league, such as Hiero, Masinissa, or the Aetolians ; they could make forced levies among subject tribes, such as the Ligurians, Gauls, or Spaniards ; or, finally, they could imitate their opponents and raise mercenaries, although they might save their pride by including such contingents as ' allies '. In fact all these sources were freely drawn on during the first half of the second century b.c., and all troops of this kind were known as *auxilia*, to distinguish them from the *socii* of the old organization. This at any rate seems to be the distinction recognized by the grammarians, and it agrees generally with the terminology employed by Livy, who may be supposed in such a matter to be following his sources. A good example both of republican methods and of the phraseology employed may be found in Livy's elaborate description of the measures taken to make up the army required for the Macedonian campaign of 171 b.c. : ' P. Licinio consuli ad exercitum civilem socialemque petenti addita auxilia Ligurum duo milia, Cretenses sagittarii—incertus numerus, quantum rogati auxilia Cretenses misissent, Numidae item equites elephantique.' Of the troops grouped here under the heading of *auxilia* the Numidians represent a contingent sent by an independent ally, Masinissa, the Ligurians were probably obtained by a forced levy, while the Cretans, nominally allies, may fairly be described as mercenaries. That their services were hardly disinterested is shown by the fact that in the following year the Senate found it necessary to issue a sharp warning to the Cretan states against their habit of supplying contingents to both sides. The fact that the Roman star was now definitely in the ascendant probably reconciled the Cretans to this interference with their national customs, for from this date onward Cretan regiments regularly form a part of the republican armies; it will be remembered that the Senate made use of a body of Cretan archers against the followers of Caius Gracchus, and a similar corps is found serving under Caesar in his second Gallic campaign.

The course of the second century saw the auxilia still more firmly established as an essential part of the republican military system. Before its close the Roman and Italian cavalry had entirely disappeared; the changes in the condition of military service, in particular the tedious and unprofitable Spanish campaigns, made the members of the upper classes, among whom the cavalry had been recruited, increasingly reluctant to take their places in the ranks as private soldiers. After the reforms of Marius the legion had no cavalry attached to it, and if the Italian contingents still existed they must likewise have disappeared when, in consequence of the extension of the franchise ino and 89 b.c., the former *socii* were all enrolled in the legions. From this moment the Roman generals depended for their cavalry upon the auxilia alone. In the case of the light-armed troops the same process took place, although here military rather than political reasons probably predominated. The last recorded use of the *velites*, the old national light infantry, is during the war against Iugurtha, and they were probably abolished by Marius. There is certainly no instance of any but auxiliaries being employed as light troops during the following century. From these considerations it necessarily follows that when, during the last fifty years of the Republic, a standing army came into existence, a number of auxiliary regiments formed part of it. When Caesar mentions that he had Cretan archers, Balearic slingers, and Numidian cavalry under his command so early as the beginning of his second campaign, we can hardly doubt that these regiments had formed part of the regular troops which he found in the province.

Thus before the end of the Republic we have the chief feature of the military system of the Empire, the division of the army into the legions of *cives Romani* and the auxiliary light troops and cavalry supplied by the unenfranchised provincials, already in existence. Even the practice of conferring the *civitas* upon troops of this class as a reward for military service was resorted to by the Republic, although probably only under exceptional conditions. We possess a document recording a grant of this nature to some Spanish auxiliaries, members of a *turma Salluitana* which had distinguished itself at the siege of Asculum in 89 b.c.

There is no evidence, however, that this branch of the service escaped the effects of the inefficiency in administration which characterized the last generation of the republican régime. Certainly too few regiments of this class were kept on a permanent footing, and a general of the period either had to take the field with far too small a proportion of cavalry and light infantry, or make up the deficiency by hasty levies called out in the districts nearest to the scene of operations. Caesar, for example, started the campaign of 58 b.c. with a totally insufficient number of regular auxiliaries, and during the following years was forced to make up his deficiency in cavalry by demanding contingents, which were often of more than doubtful fidelity, from the Gallic tribes which successively submitted to his arms. To supplement these he also raised a corps of German mercenaries and largely increased it later after the defection of the majority of the Gallic contingents to Vercingetorix.

The civil wars saw a large increase in the numbers of the auxilia. Caesar set the example by leading off thousands of his Gallic cavalry, with the object, doubtless, of using them as hostages for their compatriots' fidelity as well as of increasing his army. Pompeius followed suit and endeavoured to make up for the loss of the Italian recruiting ground by enrolling auxilia from the Eastern provinces in large numbers. The Gallic cavalry proved a great success ; in the campaign of Thapsus they showed marked superiority to the African light horse, previously accounted supreme in cavalry warfare, and the death of Caesar found them still serving in large numbers in every part of the Empire. At least those who are found, together with Lusitanians and Spaniards, in the army of Brutus and Cassius during the Philippi campaign must have been stationed either in Macedonia or the East before hostilities began.

We can thus see that when the battle of Actium in 31 b.c. placed the forces of the Roman world in the hands of Augustus, the main lines on which the military system of the Empire was based were already clearly marked, and his great work of reorganization, while importing everywhere order and principle into existing practice, I involved no breach with the military traditions of the past. To say this is in no sense to minimize his achievement. It must be remembered that while individual generals, such as Lucullus, Pompeius, or Caesar, had brought their armies to a high pitch of efficiency, the ᴏᴘ general military administration of the late republic had been chaotic in the extreme. Here, as elsewhere, the real issues were resolutely evaded, and in case of need a crisis had to be met by hasty and inefficient improvisation. Although a standing army had existed in practice for fifty years it was never accepted in principle, and no attempt was made to assess the military requirements of the state and see that an efficient force of the proper strength was maintained.   With similar lack of foresight the Senate refused to admit the principle of granting a donative on discharge, while repeatedly granting it under pressure, thus weakening the control of the central government over troops in the field and increasing the chances of a military *pronunciamento*. In consequence, the wars of this period almost invariably begin with disasters in the field, owing to the inadequacy of the standing army both in numbers and efficiency, and end with a political crisis of greater or less magnitude over the donative grievance, which naturally gave an ambitious general an opportunity of using the support of his troops to further his own ends. The work of Augustus in bringing order out of this chaos, providing forces adequate to the needs of the state, and re-establishing over them the control of the central government, is not the least of his administrative triumphs.

As a preliminary he accepted, as was perhaps inevitable, I the principle of a standing army of professional soldiers. This step has of late been severely criticized, especially by admirers of the Continental system, but it is difficult to see how short-service levies could have proved adequate to the defence of frontiers which were, for all practical purposes, more distant from Rome than Peshawur is from Aldershot. The other alternative, to entrust the provincials with the defence of their own borders, was not in harmony with his general policy, nor, it may be said, was the time ripe for such a step. The words which the third-century historian and administrator, Dio Cassius, puts into the mouth of Maecenas in dealing with this question were written doubtless with reference to the conditions of his own time, but they may certainly be applied to the earlier period, and in essence they still hold good to-day. ' You will be wise to maintain a permanent force (στρατιώτας ἀθανάτους) raised from the citizens, the subjects, and the allies distributed throughout all the provinces in larger or smaller bodies, as necessity requires. These troops must always remain in arms and be drilled constantly; at the most suitable points they must prepare themselves winter quarters, and they must serve for a fixed period calculated to allow them a little freedom after their discharge before old age comes on. For we can no longer rely upon forces called out for the occasion, owing to the distance which separates us from the borders of our Empire and the enemies which we have upon every side. If we allow all our subjects who arc of military age to possess arms and undergo a military training, there will be a continual series of riots and civil wars, while if, on the other hand, we check all military activity on their part, we shall run the risk of finding nothing but raw and untrained troops when we need a contingent for our assistance.'

The solution which Augustus found for this problem was then to revise the military system so that, while using as much as possible of the available material, he did not disturb the political conditions on which the equilibrium of the State depended. For it was no part of his intention materially to alter the structure of the Empire as an aggregate of states possessed of greater or less powers of self-government, held together by their subordination to Rome and withheld by their position from any independent external policy. Whatever possi-bilities he may have contemplated for the future he made himself few attempts to further the process of unification either by reducing the inhabitants of the privileged states to a lower grade or by the more generous policy of making wide extensions of the franchise and creating by this means a new imperial citizenship. This difference of status among the inhabitants of the Empire was naturally reflected in the military system. The *cives Romani*—that is to say, the inhabitants of Italy and of the few enfranchised communities among the provinces—furnished the new Household Troops, and the greater part, at any rate, of the recruits for the legions, and paid for their superior position as the ruling race by contributing much I more heavily in proportion to their numbers than any other class in the population. The nominally independent monarchs of the client kingdoms were allowed and encouraged to maintain armies, often of considerable size, under their own control, and frequently led in person the contingents which they were called upon to bring to the aid of the regular troops when hostilities were taking place near their borders. These contingents were often numerous and capable of rendering valuable service. Thus Rhoemetalces of Thrace assisted in the suppression of the dangerous Pannonian revolt of 6-9, and Ptolemaeus of Mauretania was publicly honoured for his loyal cooperation against the African rebel Tacfarinas. Along the eastern frontier, kingdoms of this type, the wreckage of the old Hellenistic system, were more numerous and played a more important part. Thus Antiochus III of Commagene, Agrippa II, Sohaemus of Emesa, and Malchus of Damascus contributed 15,000 men to the army which Vespasian led into Palestine in the spring of 67. Even the more autonomous city states seem to have retained a militia which was occasionally made use of. So late as the reign of Hadrian, in the army which Arrian led against the Alani, we find a contingent from the ' free ' city of Trapezus, which is reckoned among the σύμμαχοι as opposed to the regular imperial troops. A similar freedom from the direct control of Roman officers was permitted to the chiefs of some of the border tribes, who were allowed to lead their own clansmen to battle. To this type of militia belong the *tumultuariae catervae Germanorum eis Rhenum colentium*, including the Batavians under their *dux* Chariovalda, who serve in the campaigns of Germanicus, and the levies of the Dalmatian clans who started the rebellion of 6.

Last come the permanently embodied regiments raised from the subject communities, the auxilia properly so called, who form the subject of this treatise. Here, probably more than in any other department of the military system of the Empire, we can trace the results of Augustus's own activity. Regiments of this kind had, as we have seen, existed under the Republic, but they had probably been few in number and the incidence of the levy had been uneven and capricious. Under Augustus not only was the number of regiments largely increased— ' we hear of no less than fourteen alae and seventy cohorts taking part in the Pannonian War of 6-9—but the inscriptions show us that, with the exception of Greece, always the spoiled child of Roman sentiment, every quarter of the Empire contributed its quota. Details respecting the incidence of this levy on different provinces, and the methods of organization and recruiting, will be found in later sections. It will be sufficient to say here that while the subject communities had probably more reason than any other class to complain of the military demands of the state, the burden was at least more equitably distributed than under the Republic and the total contribution required, in most cases at any rate, not excessive. It is natural to suppose that the fixing of the quota supplied by each community was connected with the drawing up of the census, which placed the taxation of the Empire for the first time on an organized basis, and it seems probable that more evidence might show a reciprocal variation between the two forms of contribution required. We know, for instance, that the Batavians were altogether excused from the payment of tribute on account of the size and value of their contingent, and this case was probably not exceptional.

In all this it is easy to see how much Augustus owes to the institutions of the Republic, and when we come to consider details his debt becomes even more apparent. A standing army consisting of legions of *cives Romani* and smaller units of *peregrini,* supported in the field by contingents from allied and nominally independent states, was already in existence. His task was merely to introduce such changes as might obviate the mistakes and failures of the past, and to establish principles which should make for permanence and stability. For in accepting the principle of maintaining a standing army Augustus could not have been blind to the political dangers which this institution brought with it. He endeavoured to meet them by fixing the conditions of service, in particular the sum which a soldier might claim at his discharge, and by establishing a special treasury from which those claims might be satisfied, thus accustoming the troops to look to the central government, not to their generals, for rewards due to them. Moreover, in this department of the state even Augustus allowed no respect for constitutional forms to veil or weaken his authority. When in 69 the legions on the Upper Rhine tore down the *imagines* of Galba and swore allegiance to the *oblitterata iam nomina senatus populique Romani* it was a manifest sign that after a century of peace a new period of anarchy had begun. Since this military system, with its division of the troops into categories differing from each other in status and prestige, reflected the general conditions prevalent in the Empire, so it was inevitable that a change in these conditions should have its effect also upon the army. How far the political developments of the first century were foreseen or intended by Augustus it is perhaps impossible to say; it is certain, at any rate, that his system was capable of adapting itself to them. One of these developments was a steady increase in the power of the central government and a disappearance of all forms of local autonomy which involved a division of authority. By the reign of Vespasian almost all the great client kingdoms had been more or less peaceably absorbed into the ordinary provincial system. Cappadocia was annexed in7, Mauretania in 39, Thrace in 46, Pontus in 63, and Commagene in 73. The troops which these kingdoms had maintained were naturally taken into the Roman service, transformed into auxiliary regiments, and lost the privilege which attached to their former condition of serving only in local campaigns. One instance of such a transference, in the case of a regiment which had been in the service of the kings of Pontus, is mentioned in Tacitus, and we also meet with Hemeseni on the Danube, Commageni in Africa and Noricum, and the successors of one of Herod's old Samaritan regiments in Mauretania. The resentment with which the new conditions of service were sometimes received is an instructive comment on the wisdom of Augustus's policy in not enforcing their universal applica-bility at an earlier date. The Thracians, for example, rose in open revolt when they were first summoned to supply a contingent for service at a distance from their own borders. Somewhat similar was the fate of the border militia on the Rhine and Danube. On the latter frontier the revolt of 6-9 showed at an early date the dangers of the system. After its suppression the clan chiefs seem, in many cases at any rate, to have been deposed and replaced by Roman officials, regiments of Pannonians and Dalmatians were raised and transferred to other provinces, and a garrison was imported from outside to control the country. On the Rhine the process was a more gradual one. The Batavi, for example, whom we have noticed serving in the campaigns of Germanicus as a clan levy under their *dux* Chariovalda, seem to have been organized in regular auxiliary regiments by the middle of the first century, although they still retained, in common with many other corps of Rhenish auxilia, their clan chiefs as their *praefecti*. In the year 69 we also find the Helvetii still responsible for maintaining the garrison of a fort within their borders, and a militia existing in Raetia capable of supplementing the garrison of regular auxilia. Some even of the Gallic states, which were more distant from the frontier, sent contingents to support Vitellius, which were not, however, regarded as a very sensible addition to his forces.

Probably these last vestiges of independent organization and control were swept away at the time of the reorganization of the Rhine army in 70, after the rebellion of Civilis. From this date onward there are at any rate few traces here or elsewhere of any use of irregulars of this type by the military authorities. This militia, which might have proved invaluable in the days to come as a national reserve, fell a victim, together with the local autonomy on which it was based, to the growing tendency towards centralization which marks the first and second centuries. The super-session of local officials by the agents of a centralized bureaucracy in the civil administration coincides with the complete transference of the burden of the defence of the state to the shoulders of a professional army. It is the purpose of the following chapters to discuss one part of this army, the auxilia, to trace its organization and the part which it played in frontier defence, and to illustrate from this study the lines on which the military system of the Empire developed and the causes of its failure.

THE AUXILIA DURING THE FIRST TWO CENTURIES A.D.

SECTION I.THE STRENGTH AND ORGANIZATION OF THE AUXILIARY REGIMENTS

From the death of Augustus to the period when the frontier defences first began to collapse under the strain of the barbarian invasions, more than two centuries later, the imperial army presents a picture of military con-servatism unrivalled in history. Not only does the original distinction between the legions of *civ es Romani* I and the auxilia of *peregrini* remain throughout the basis of its organization, but even individual corps show a marvellous power of vitality. Dio Cassius, writing at the beginning of the third century, notes that, of the twenty-five legions in existence in4, eighteen still survived in his own day, and epigraphical evidence shows that scores even of the more easily destructible auxiliary regiments could claim as long a record. In appearance, indeed, the only considerable change introduced into the organization of the auxilia during this period was the addition of the *numeri* in the second century to the *alae* and *cohortes* which had previously been the only units employed. It is true, of course, that this conservatism was in some respects rather superficial, and that, while administrative forms and nomenclature remained unaltered, in more essential matters the army had been deeply affected by the tendencies of the age. It is still, however, possible, while paying due attention to these changes, to treat the two centuries which follow the death of Augustus as a single period in the history of the auxilia ; it is only amid the confusion caused by the barbarian invasions of the third century and the subsequent attempts at reorganization that we definitely lose sight of our old landmarks.

Leaving out of account for the moment the *numeri*, which, as late creations with a special significance, are reserved for future discussion, let us commence with the *alae* and *cohortes*, which remained throughout this period the units of auxiliary cavalry and infantry respectively.

Both these terms, although their history is widely different, originate in the military terminology of the Republic. The term *cohors* had been originally applied to the infantry contingents of the Italian *socii*, which were not united in legions after the model of the levies of *cives Romani*, and it was naturally retained after the disappearance of the *socii* to describe the similar tactical units of provincial auxilia.

The term *ala* originated as a metaphorical description of the two divisions into which the contingents of *socii* were formed, which were stationed in the normal republican order of battle on either flank of the legions. After the disappearance of the *socii* the term was applied in a more restricted sense to the two flanking divisions in which the average Roman general massed all his available cavalry. This use of the word continued down to the last days of the Republic. When, for instance, the author of the *De bello Africo* writes, ' Caesar *alteram* alam mittit qui satagentibus celeriter occurreret,' or Cicero says of his son in the *De Officiis*, ' Quo tarnen in hello cum te Pompeius *alteri* alae praefecisset, magnam laudem et a summo viro, et abexercitu conscquebare equitando, iaculando . . .,' the word is clearly being used in this sense, and does not refer to a regiment of any fixed size. In fact the cavalry of the *socii* never seem to have been organized in larger units than *turmae*, and the auxiliary levies naturally adopted the same formation. It has already been noticed that some of the Spanish auxiliaries who served in the Social War are officially described as belonging to a *turma Salluitana*. Occasional phrases in Livy, such as the statement that the Aetolian cavalry contingent, in the campaign of 171 b.c., was *alae unius instar*, do not seem to prove anything more than that the historian used the technical terms of his own age to make his narrative clearer. This usage, however, shows that Livy was familiar with the restricted meaning of the word—that is to say, the ala must have been a recognized institution in the reign of Augustus, and we may add that Velleius states that fourteen alae were employed in the Pannonian campaigns of 6-9 in which he himself had served.

It is improbable, however, that the ala was a creation of Augustus, although he may have determined its exact size and organization. In Caesar's account of his Gallic campaigns we find frequent mention of contingents of tribal cavalry serving as independent units under officers bearing the title of *praefecti equitum*, and these units must have been much larger than *turmae*. The organization of these regiments, originally of a purely temporary kind, must have been placed on a more permanent basis when many of them were taken out of their own country to serve in the Civil Wars, and it would have been natural that a new term should be used to describe them.

Evidence in support of this conjecture, which is, as we have seen, lacking in the writings of Caesar and his continuators, has been sought for elsewhere. The majority of Caesar's *praefecti equitum* seem to have been tribal chiefs ; one may cite, for example, the Aeduan Dumnorix, the heroic veteran Vertiscus, and the two treacherous Allobroges, Roucillus and Egus, the sons of Adbucillus. On the other hand, when we meet with an ala Scaevae on an early inscription, it is difficult to avoid agreeing with Mommsen that it was called after Caesar's well-known officer of that name. Many other cavalry regiments, which are shown by epigraphical evidence to have existed at an early date and to have been Gallic in composition, bear titles similarly formed from personal names. It is suggested that these corps, or at any rate the majority of them, represent tribal contingents embodied by Caesar at the time of the Civil Wars under the title of *alae* and placed under his veteran officers. Thus during this period the use of the term *ala* in the restricted sense would be already known, although only the older and wider use appears in literature. How slowly the new expression won favour is shown by the fact that during the reigns of Augustus and Tiberius the officers commanding these regiments were usually described on inscriptions simply as *praefectus equitum*, and it was not until after this that the title *praefectus alae* came to be generally adopted.

Curiously enough, we find very few cohorts with titles which suggest a similar history. Probably in this case Augustus's reorganization was more thorough and the existing regiments had not, like some of Caesar's corps of Gallic cavalry, a record of individual achievement which might exempt them from its scope.

Size of regiments. In discussing the size of the auxiliary regiments we have two questions to settle, the numbers of the establishment and the actual strength at which the regiments were maintained. As regards the first question, the evidence of Hyginus and the inscriptions shows us that both *alae* and *cohortes* were known as *miliariae* or *quingenariae*—that is to say, they contained, roughly speaking, 500 or 1,000 men each. The smaller unit seems to have been preferred in the first century, while the larger predominates among the corps raised by Trajan and his successors. The exact theoretical size, both of the regiments themselves and of the centuries and *turmae* into which they were divided, is more difficult to determine. Hyginus states that an *ala quingenaria* was divided into sixteen *turmae*, and an *ala miliaria* into twenty-four. He does not state the number of men in a *turma* in either case, and it seems impossible to arrive at any certainty on the basis of figures found elsewhere in his treatise. Turning to epigraphical evidence we find an inscription from Coptos which describes the composition of a *vexillatio* drawn from three alae and seven cohorts, as: ' Alarum III: dec(uriones) V, dupl(icarius) I, sesquiplic(arii) IIII, equites CCCCXXIIII. Cohortium VII: centuriones X, eq(uites) LXI, mil(ites) DCCLXXXIIX '. Von Domaszewski suggests that the cavalry in this detachment are to be divided into ten *turmae* of 42 men, each commanded by a *decurio*, a *duplicarius*, or a *sesquiplicarius*, and that this figure represents the theoretical strength of the *turma* in an *ala miliaria*. In an *ala quingenaria*, on the other hand, the *turma* probably contained only o men.

This seems to be as near certainty as we are likely to arrive in the present state of our evidence, unless indeed we take literally a statement of Arrian that an *ala* contained 512 men, a total which would presumably give 32 men to the *turma*. Arrian is, of course, the best authority on the imperial army whom we possess, but the remark in question is a parenthesis inserted into an account of the ideal establishment of a Hellenistic army, and he may have meant no more than that the unit under discussion corresponded roughly with a Roman *ala quingenaria*. More satisfactory and conclusive evidence will perhaps be found when the barracks of an ala in a frontier fort have been accurately planned.

The size of the auxiliary cohorts is a matter of even greater difficulty. Hyginus states, and there seems no reason to doubt his statement, that a *cohors miliaria* was divided into ten centuries, a *cohors quingenaria* into six. Archaeological evidence supports this statement and suggests further that the centuries were in each case of the same size, since the centurial barracks in the fort at Housesteads, in Northumberland, which was occupied by a *cohors miliaria*, offer almost precisely the same accommodation as those in the Scottish fort at Newstead, which are clearly designed to accommodate two *cohortes quingenariae*. The question to be decided is whether these centuries contained 80 or 100 men each. In either case, one of the titles must be a misnomer, since six centuries of 100 would make a *cohors quingenaria* consist of 600 men, while ten centuries of 80 would only give 800 men for a *cohors miliaria*. On the whole, although Hyginus suggests the higher figure, the lower is probably to be preferred. Certainly the Coptos inscription cited above, which is probably the most valuable evidence which we possess, clearly indicates centuries of 80. The most important evidence on the other side is that of Josephus, who describes some cohorts which belonged to the Syrian army in 67 a.d. as containing ἀνὰ χίλιους πεζούς. His succeeding statement, however, that other cohorts, by which *cohortes equitatae quingenariae* are apparently meant, contained 600 infantry and 120 cavalry, suggests that he may be basing his reckoning simply on the number of centuries. Few would defend his calculation in the second instance, and he may be equally wrong in the first. On the whole, therefore, it seems safer to assume establishments of 480 and 800 men for *cohortes quingenariae* and *miliariae* respectively, although it remains, of course, possible that the size of the cohorts was altered between the Jewish war of 66-70 and the period of the erection of those frontier forts upon which we have been relying for our evidence.

The last question to be settled in this connexion is that of the *cohortes equitatae*, in which a proportion of the men were mounted, which form a peculiar and interesting feature of the imperial army. Corps in which infantry and cavalry fought together had of course always been common, but the idea was probably revived by the" 'Romans from observing the practice of the German tribes, from whom Julius obtained a contingent accustomed to fight in this manner. It is certainly significant that one of the earliest of these regiments known to us from inscriptions is a *cohors Ubiorum*. There is, however, no later evidence for the employment of these tactics, and the continued use of *cohortes equitatae* is due rather to the necessity of having detachments of mounted men at as many frontier stations as possible. The *equites cohortales* should be reckoned rather as mounted infantry than cavalry, since we learn from a fragment of Hadrian's address to the army in Africa that they were worse mounted than the *equites alares*, and less skilled in cavalry manœuvres. As regards the strength of these regiments and the proportion of mounted to unmounted men, Hyginus states that the *cohors miliaria equitata* contained 760 infantry and 240 cavalry, while the *cohors quingenaria* contained six centuries, and in other respects, ' *in dimidio eandem rationem continet* '—that is to say, it apparently had 380 infantry and 120 cavalry. The figures for the mounted men are probably correct, and, since we learn from an inscription that there were four decurions to a *cohors quingenaria*, we may presume that the *turmae* were 30 strong. This agrees very well with the Egyptian vexillation cited above, which included 61 *equites cohortales*—that is to say, 2 *turmae*. On the other hand, there is considerable reason for supposing that the figures for the infantry are schematic and incorrect. It is sufficient here to remark that centuries of 76 could not be divided into *contubernia* of either 8 or 10, and that the 380 men of Hyginus's *cohors quingenaria* could not even be divided evenly among six centuries. The question cannot be settled with certainty until forts occupied by regiments of this class have been planned, but it seems probable that while the number of the centuries remained unaltered the complement of each was reduced from 80 to 60, or possibly to 64, if it was thought desirable to retain the division into *contubernia* of 8.

Having endeavoured to determine the theoretical establishment of the auxiliary regiments, it remains to discover how far this corresponded to the actual strength at which they were maintained, and here our evidence is scanty, and likely to remain so. Fortunately, the discovery in Egypt of some of the official papers of the Cohors I Augusta Praetoria Lusitanorum has thrown some light on the question. On January 1, 156, this regiment had on its books 6 centurions, 3 decurions, 114 mounted infantry, 19 camel-riders (*dromedarii*), and 363 infantry, making, with the *praefectus*, a total of 506 men. Between January and May, 18 recruits were enrolled, 15 infantry, an *eques*, a *dromedarius*, and a decurion. These figures agree fairly well with the arrangement suggested above, although the *dromedarii* are an additional complication, and the regiment appears even to have exceeded its 'paper-strength'. This, however, may be easily accounted for if we imagine that a number of men had served their term and were about to be discharged. Unfortunately, this document remains isolated, and further evidence is not likely to be forthcoming.

Conditions of service. Questions concerning the method of enlistment for the auxiliary regiments are reserved, on account of their connexion with the broader issues raised by the whole recruiting system, for discussion in a later section. For the present it will be sufficient to discuss the conditions of service in this branch of the army, as they are laid down in the so-called *diplomata militaria*. These documents, of which we possess some 70 or 80 examples dealing with the auxilia, are small bronze tablets, issued originally to individual soldiers, recording the privileges granted to them either after their discharge or after they had completed a term of 25 years. The reason for this variation seems to be that while the *praemia militiae* were always conferred after the regulation number of years had been served, it was often the practice to retain the men with the colours for some years longer before finally discharging them. This practice, which we hear of in the early empire as a standing grievance of the legionaries, seems to have prevailed also among the auxilia during the first century. After 107, however, we have no instances of the *praemia* unpreceded by discharge, a change which is probably due to the perfection of organization, and can be traced also in the legions.

Previous to the reign of Antoninus Pius, the privileges granted to the recipient of a diploma include citizenship for himself, the full legalization of any matrimonial union into which he has entered or shall enter in the future (*conubium*), and civic rights for his wife, children, and descendants. If he already possessed a family, the names of his wife and children follow his own on the diploma, and the frequency of this occurrence shows the extent to which the military authorities permitted the soldiers to form family ties while on active service. The significance of this fact and its effect on the character of the army will be discussed in a later section.

At the beginning of the reign of Antoninus Pius, a change takes place in that part of the formula which concerns the grant of citizenship. In place of the words *ipsis liberis posterisque cor urn civitatem dedit et conubium cum uxoribus*, &c, we read in all the later examples, *civitatem Romanam, qui eorum non haberent, dedit et conubium cum uxoribus*, &c. The first inference to be drawn from this alteration is that there now existed a numerous group of auxiliary soldiers who possessed the *civitas* before their discharge, and we are probably justified in the further inference that many actually possessed it when they were enrolled. It has been noted, for example, that on a document dating from the reign of Trajan, six recruits accepted for the Cohors III Ituraeorum all have the *tria nomina*. In this change, I then, we have a clear instance of the extent to which the franchise was now diffused throughout the Empire.

The omission of the phrase *liberis -posterisque eorum*, on the other hand, suggests the opposite tendency. It cannot, of course, mean that children born after their father's discharge would not be *cives*, for their status would be secured by the grant of *conubium*, but it seems clear that those born before it no longer acquired the citizenship with him. This is supported not only by the absence of all mention of children on the later diplomata, but by the phraseology of an Egyptian document dealing with an ἐπίκρισις of the year 148 which distinguishes two classes of veterans, ἔνειοὶ μὲν ἐπιτυχόντες σὺν τέκνοις καὶ ἐγγόνοις, ἕτεροι μόνοι τῆς Ῥωμαίων ποτειτείας (sic) καὶ ἐπιγαμίας πρὸς γυναῖκας ἃς τότε εἶχον, ὅτε τούτοις ἡ πολιτεία ἐδόθη, &c. Clearly we have here a translation of both types of formula, and the translator gave to the second the same meaning as that suggested above. Clearly, too, the change was considered an important one since the veterans discharged before and after it are thus divided into two groups. In view of the prevailing policy of the imperial government with respect to the extension of the *civitas* this step has a curiously retrograde appearance, and it is difficult to see the motives which suggested it. Possibly it was merely desired to get rid of an anomalous situation by which the auxiliaries had previously occupied a more privileged position than the Household Troops. In any case, even after this restriction, there can be little doubt that the grant of the *civitas* with the improvement in civil status which it brought to the recipient, and the increased possibilities which it offered to his children, must have done much to popularize the service. We have seen that the idea of such a reward did not originate with the Empire, but it was probably not until the reorganization of the army by Augustus that it was regularly conferred and the years of service required to earn it definitely fixed.

We do not know whether at the time of their discharge the auxiliaries also received, like the legionaries, a grant of money or land in lieu of a pension. It seems certain that their status excluded them from a share in the *donativa*, which the emperors distributed among the troops at their accession, and on other special occasions, and that they could only receive the *dona militaria* after a special preliminary grant of the civitas. That such grants were made, even to whole regiments at a time, is shown by the number of cohorts which commemorate the receipt of this honour by employing the title *civium Romanorum*.

On the still more important matter of the ordinary pay of the auxiliary regiments an almost equal uncertainty prevails. Our only two pieces of evidence on the subject, a passage in Tacitus and a phrase in Hadrian's address to the garrison of Africa, tell us nothing more than that the *equites cohortales* were paid on a higher scale than the infantry, but received in their turn less than the *equites alares*, a preference in favour of the mounted men, which is not so great as appears at first sight, since it is clear that they were responsible for the upkeep of their own horses. The chief defect of these passages is that they do not mention the amount of the pay in any of the three cases. Our only basis for calculation is the fact that a legionary considered it promotion to be made *duplicarius alae*; hence the pay of an ordinary cavalryman must have been more than half that of a legionary. On *a priori* considerations it can hardly have been less, if, as Hadrian's speech suggests, he paid for his own arms and mount, and if he also, like the legionaries, had the cost of his rations deducted from his pay. On the whole, however, it seems best to defer speculation until further evidence is forthcoming.

Internal organization. As is only natural in the case of a professional army with so long a term of service, the internal organization of the auxiliary regiments reveals a far more complicated system of grades and promotions than anything which the ancient world had yet known. The epigraphical evidence is abundant, and the efforts of modern scholars, particularly von Domaszewski in his monumental treatise, *Die Rangordnung des römischen Heeres*, have done much to make the main lines of the system clear. Difficulties in detail still remain, but we may hope for their ultimate solution.

The commanding officer of an *ala quingenaria* or *miliaria*, or of a *cohors quingenaria* bore the title of ' *praefectus*. *Cohortes miliariae* and the *cohortes civium Romanorum*, which occupied an exceptional position, were commanded by *tribuni*. Early inscriptions also mention a *subpraefectus alae* and a *subpraefectus cohortis*, but these posts seem later to have been abandoned. In later times in case of the absence of the *praefectus*, his place seems to have been filled by an officer placed temporarily in charge with the title of *praepositus* or *curator*. Questions concerning the order of precedence among the *praefecti* and *tribuni*, and their place in the military hierarchy generally, are so closely connected with the method of selection and appointment of these officers at different periods, that they are best left for future discussion. It is only important here to note that they usually entered the service with this rank, and that it is very rare to find the regular commander either of an ala or cohort drawn from among the lower officers.

The remaining ' commissioned officers ', as we should call them, are represented by the troop and company commanders, the decurions who commanded the *turmae* of the ala, and the centurions and decurions of the cohorts. The senior officer in each class was styled *decurio princeps* or *centurio princeps*, but apart from this we cannot trace any regular order of precedence with fixed titles such as is found among the legionary centurions. As regards the respective position of infantry and cavalry officers, the *decurio alae* ranked highest. This is shown clearly, as von Domaszewski has pointed out, by the frequent employment of this officer as *praepositus cohortis*. On the other hand, among the officers of the cohorts the centurions ranked above the decurions who commanded the mounted men, where such existed. In one inscription, which seems to have included all the officers of a *cohors equitata*, the centurions come first on the list, and in the Coptos inscription, so often cited, the officers of the 61 *equites cohortales* are not mentioned at all. The difference in rank cannot, however, have been very great since all these officers could be promoted to the post of legionary centurion without any intervening step, although this distinction seems to have been conferred most freely upon the decurions of the alae. In these cases it was of course necessary for the auxiliary officer to have acquired the *civitas* either by serving his full time or by a special grant before his promotion.

Throughout the period these posts seem usually to have been filled by promotion from the lower ranks, although we also find instances of legionaries being given commissioned rank in the auxiliary regiments, and it is officers of this class who seem most frequently to have secured further promotion to the legionary centurionate. Von Domaszewski wishes to consider that these transfers were especially characteristic of the early days of the imperial army, and that a deliberate attempt was then made to provide every auxiliary regiment with a staff of ex-legionaries. With this suggestion, however, it is difficult to agree; not only is the epigraphical evidence insufficient to prove such a wholesale use of imported officers, but the cases known to us are by no means confined to the first fifty years of the Empire. Further, as will be shown later, the arrangement does not harmonize with the general character of the early *auxilia*.

The holders of subordinate posts, who ranked below the centurion or decurion, may be divided, following the arrangement adopted by von Domaszewski, into two groups. The members of the first group practically correspond to our non-commissioned officers, and are able to command small detachments or to take the place, if necessary, of the company officers. These alone, and the holders of certain higher administrative posts, to which the *taktische Chargen* gave access, have a legitimate claim to the title of *principales*. The members of the second group did not, strictly speaking, rank above the privates, but they were granted freedom from certain routine duties in return for special services which they discharged, and were distinguished in consequence by the title of *immunes*.

It is of course often difficult to ascertain whether a particular post falls into the higher or lower group, and this is especially the case with the standard-bearers, who occupy a position of peculiar importance in the military system. In the ala each troop had its own flag carried by the *signifer turmae*, but there seems also to have been a regimental standard, the bearer of which was known as

the *vexillarius alae*. A few inscriptions also mention an *imaginifer*, but it is not clear whether this officer always or at all periods found a place on the staff. In a cohort, on the other hand, each century seems to have had its *signifer*, and each turma of mounted men its *vexillarius*, but it does not appear that there was a regimental standard, any more than there existed at this date a standard for each cohort of a legion. This at least is implied by Tacitus in his description of the entry of the Vitellian army into Rome, when he mentions the *alarum signa* by the side of the *legionum aquilae*, but says nothing of the ensigns of the cohorts. We must suppose, then, that the *imaginifer cohortis*, who is mentioned on inscriptions, was not regarded as the regimental standard-bearer any more than the *imaginifer legionis*.

In consequence of this difference in organization the company and troop standard-bearers of the cohorts rank among the *principales*, while in the alae only the regimental standard-bearer is included in the higher group, and the *signiferi turmae* sink to the position of *immunes*.

Returning, then, to the ala we may place at the head of the *principales* the *vexillarius*, and next to him the *imaginifer*, when this officer existed. Other members of this class were the non-commissioned officers of every turma, the *duplicarius* and *sesquiplicarius*, who derived their titles from the fact that they were paid twice and one and a half times the private's pay respectively, an institution found in the Hellenistic military system from which it was probably borrowed. Lastly we should perhaps add the *optio*, who commanded the escort of the *praefectus (singulares)*.

To the lower group, the *immunes*, belong the *signifer, custos armorum,* and *curator* attached to every turma, the *cornicularius, actarius, strator, stator, librarius,* and *beneficiarius,* who form the clerical and administrative staff of the *praefectus,* and his escort, the *singulares.* In determining the position of the holders of these posts among the *immunes* we are supported by the analogy of the Equites Singulares Imperatoris, a corps modelled upon and to a certain extent recruited from the auxiliary cavalry. The list of a *turma* of this regiment contained on a Roman inscription gives the following arrangement :

> nomina turmae
> Iul(ius) Mascel(lus) dec(urio)
> Nonius Severus dup(licarius)
> Iul(ius) Victorinus sesq(uiplicarius)
> Aur(elius) Mucatral Aur(elius) Lucius
> Ael(ius) Crescens sig(nifer)
> Aur(elius) Victor arm(orum custos)
> Aur(elius) Atero cur(ator)
> Ael(ius) Victor bf (beneficiarius)
> Cl(audius) Victorinus lib(rarius)
> Iul(ius) Vindex bf (beneficiarius)
> 17 names of equites follow.

The fact that two privates occupy the fourth and fifth places shows clearly that the holders of all the posts mentioned lower in the list belong to the *immunes.* Had it not been for this piece of evidence we might have been tempted to place the *signifer turmae* in the higher category. The analogy of the Equites Singulares also suggests that we may include the *bucinator* and *tubicen* among the *immunes* of the ala, and we have also to add the *medicus,* whose somewhat exceptional position is discussed later.

A distinction between the *principales* and *immunes* of the cohorts may be based partly upon the principles already adopted for the ala, partly upon the analogy of the legion, the organization of which was clearly followed in several respects. On these grounds we may class as *principales* the *imaginifer cohortis,* the *signifer, optio,* and *tesserarius* of each century, and the *optio* and *vexillarius* of each turma in the *cohortes equitatae.* The case of the *optio,* who commanded, if necessary, in the place of the centurion or decurion, may be taken for granted. It may also be noted that both *optio* and *vexillarius* could be promoted to the position of decurion without any intervening step. The *tesserarius,* whose main duty consisted in receiving from the centurion the orders and password for the day and transmitting them to the men, is found in charge of a detachment on special duty, as is also the *imaginifer cohortis.* The *signifer* lastly, can hardly have had a position inferior to that of the *vexillarius* or *tessera-rius,* and would indeed rank higher than the latter if the analogy of the legions holds good. As regards the *immunes,* the officer commanding a cohort possessed a smaller administrative staff than the *praefectus alae,* including only the *cornicularius, actarius, librarius,* and *beneficiarius.* The musicians possibly include the *cornicen* as well as the *tubicen* and the *bucinator,* and the post of *mensor* seems to be confined to the cohorts. At least no inscription has yet mentioned one among the *immunes* of the ala.

Finally, as regards the position of the *medici,* who were attached to the cohorts as well as to the alae, a few special remarks seem necessary. On a British inscription one of these army doctors is described as *medicus Ordinarius,* which would naturally mean that he served in the ranks, and a passage in the *Digest* confirms this by ranking the *medici* among the *immunes.* On the other hand, M. Ulpius Sporus, who is described in an inscription erected by his freedmen at Ferentinum in Etruria as *medicus alae Indianae et tertiae Astorum* (sic), seems to be on rather a higher level, as also M. Rubrius Zosimus of Ostia, who was doctor to the Cohors IV Aquitanorum in Germania Superior in the second century. Both these men are apparently Greeks, and can hardly have reached their regiments by the ordinary recruiting channels. It has been noticed also that the *medici* appear to have a special position in some inscriptions of the Praetorian cohorts. Probably, then, one may infer two classes of *medici,* the common soldier who possessed some elementary qualifications (first aid and blood-letting) and was given the position of an *immunis,* and the fully-trained professional doctor who was attached to a regiment but held no actual military rank. It was probably to distinguish himself from the latter class that the *medicus* of the Tungrian cohort added the word *Ordinarius* to his title.

As regards the rate and method of promotion, and the order of precedence of the various posts within the two groups of *principales* and *immunes,* we know practically nothing. There is nothing to show that it was customary to hold several posts in a regular order, or to become an *immunis* before entering the -*principales.* It was doubtless usual for a man not to receive commissioned rank without first holding some subordinate post, but we do not know that any such preliminary qualification was essential. Owing to the length of service promotion was probably not rapid, but on the other hand the number of posts available was very large. In an *ala quingenaria,* for example, there were 16 decurions, 34 *principales,* and probably over 100 *immunes.* Thus every soldier must have felt confident of obtaining sooner or later a position of greater ease and profit, and this, together with the fact that the ladder of promotion led to commissioned rank, and even to the coveted legionary centurionate, must have increased the attractions of the profession.

Titles of the regiments. The titles of the auxiliary regiments were as various in form as those of the legions, and it is unnecessary to give a complete list of them. The alae which bear a title derived from a personal name, presumably that of their original commander, have been mentioned already. The majority of them were probably raised during Caesar's Gallic campaigns or the Civil Wars, and there are few to which a later date can be assigned with any certainty. The few cohorts known to have borne such titles are more difficult to explain, but have perhaps a similar origin. Regiments raised under the Empire, on the other hand, were usually called by the name of the tribe or district from which they were raised, and distinguished by a number from other corps of the same origin. In course of time these ethnical titles were in many cases supplemented by others, some of which were granted as marks of distinction and rewards for meritorious service, while others were purely descriptive. Examples of the former class are the title *civium Romanorum*, which indicates that on some occasion all the members of a corps received the franchise before their discharge, and honorary epithets, such as *pia, fidelis,* or *fida.* The title *Augusta* seems also to have been granted at all periods *honoris causa*, although some of the regiments bearing it may date back to the beginning of the Empire. Titles derived from the names of later emperors, on the other hand, while they were doubtless granted occasionally as marks of distinction, seem often to indicate nothing more than the reign during which a regiment was raised. Finally, from the time of Severus Antoninus onwards, every regiment employs a secondary title, derived from the name of the reigning emperor. A remarkable series of dedicatory inscriptions of the Cohors I Aelia Dacorum, which was stationed during the third century at Birdoswald (Amboglanna), on the British frontier, shows us this regiment successively assuming the titles *Antoniniana, Gordiana, Postumiana,* and *Tetriciana.*

Purely descriptive titles might be derived either from the size of the regiment *(miliaria, quingenaria),* its composition *(equitata, gemina),* its weapons *(seutata, contariorum, sagittariorum),* or the name of the province in which it was or had been stationed *(Syriaca, Moesiaca).* A frequent motive for the assumption and accumulation of such secondary descriptive titles seems to have been the desire of a regiment to distinguish itself from another unit bearing the same number and ethnical title, and stationed in the same province. This was probably the origin of the title *veterana* or *veteranorum,* which was borne by five alae and five cohorts, although its interpretation is much disputed According to von Domaszewski, these regiments were so called because they were originally formed of discharged veterans recalled to active service in time of war. Cichorius suggests that a regiment assumed this name when another corps bearing the same number and ethnical title, but of more recent origin, was stationed in the same province. This certainly furnishes the best explanation in the case of the Cohors III Thracum c. R., and the Cohors III Thracum veteranorum, which appear together in the Raetian diplomata for 107 and 166. On von Domaszewski's theory it is difficult to see why a regiment of recalled veterans should bear the number III, and his explanation that ' the numbers borne by these corps are connected with the numbering of the auxilia in the province to which they were attached after their formation from *missicii* ' does not make matters much clearer. Cichorius's suggestion would also account satisfactorily for the Cohors I Aquitanorum and the Cohors I Aquitanorum veterana, which appear together in Germania Superior in 74, and the Cohors I Claudia Sugambrorum and the Cohors I Sugambrorum veterana which were stationed together in Moesia Inferior. The latter would be identical with the regiment mentioned by Tacitus as forming part of the garrison of the province in the reign of Tiberius. In other cases where similar duplication cannot be proved it must be remembered that our evidence is very imperfect, and that a regiment after assuming this title may have continued to use it when the reason for doing so had disappeared.

These descriptive and honorary epithets, although sometimes borne alone, were usually employed to supplement the original ethnical title, with the result that after a hundred years of meritorious service the ' full style ' of a second-century regiment might be almost as long and imposing as that of the emperors whom it served. As an example, one may cite the Cohors I Breucorum quingenaria Valeria Victrix bis torquata ob virtutem appellata equitata, which formed part of the garrison of Raetia.

Relation of the auxilia to the legions. It is perhaps relevant to discuss here a point affecting the auxilia as a whole, namely, their relation to the legions in the general scheme of military organization. It is generally supposed that in those frontier armies which included both classes of troops, a group of auxiliary regiments was definitely attached to each legion, and I such phrases as ' a legion with its attendant auxiliaries ' are common in writers on the military system of the Roman Empire. Evidence as to the exact nature and even the existence of such a connexion is, however, somewhat difficult to find. Tacitus does, it is true, refer to the eight Batavian cohorts, who play such an important part in the events of 69, as *auxilia quartae decimae legionis,* but no other passage can be quoted in the same sense, and the connexion in this case was obviously neither close nor durable. In the comparatively detailed account of the first campaign of Bedriacum, which rests at any rate upon a good military source, there is no suggestion that the auxilia marched or manoeuvred in separate groups, each connected with a particular legion. Certainly in the normal order of battle throughout the first century the available auxilia were all massed together either as a first line, or in two flanking divisions to the right and left of the legionaries, and the auxilia of the army which crossed the Rhine in 73 were not divided among the legionary *legati*, but had a commander of their own.

Supporters of the legionary connexion also refer to the two diplomata issued in the same year and on the same day (August 14, 99) to two different groups of auxiliary regiments stationed in Moesia Inferior, and suggest that this curious arrangement can best be explained on the supposition that each diploma refers only to the auxilia of one legion. A similar explanation suggests itself for the fact that only one regiment is common to the two British diplomata of 103 and 105. It seems impossible, however, to interpret all the diplomata in this manner. The British diploma of 124, for example, which was issued to men from six alae and twenty-one cohorts, can hardly be supposed to contain the auxilia of only one of the three legions then stationed in the province. In Pannonia Superior also so many regiments are common to the five complete second-century diplomata which we possess that we must, on this theory, refer them all to the auxilia of one and the same legion. How, then, do we account for the fact that the inscriptions of the province hardly mention any regiments but those contained in these diplomata? In other words, why should all our evidence refer to the auxilia of one legion, and those attached to the other two, then stationed in the province, have entirety disappeared?

A stronger argument is perhaps to be found in inscriptions which contain the phrase *legio . . . et auxilia eius*. It could be wished that these texts were more numerous and more precise, but they support the supposition that some connexion existed between each legion and a definite group of auxiliary regiments better than any evidence previously adduced.   The connexion, however, must have been very slight and easily broken. Dr. Hardy has pointed out that although three out of the four legions stationed in Germania Superior in 70 left the province for good during the following thirty-five years, there is abundant evidence that nothing like the same proportion of the auxilia stationed in the province accompanied them. It is also clear that, in the second century at any rate, the number of auxilia attached to any legion was not fixed in accordance with any general principle, but depended upon the exigencies of the local situation on each frontier. A reference to the list of provincial garrisons contained in the appendix will show that whereas there are not likely to have been more than three thousand auxilia apiece to each of the three legions of Pannonia Superior, there were probably thirty thousand to be divided among the three legions of Britain, while in Dacia there was only one legion with something approaching twenty-five thousand auxilia. Still, with these reservations, it seems possible enough that the auxilia were always considered as in some sense dependent on the legions, and that where several legions were stationed in the same province, an arrangement was made dividing the auxilia into a corresponding number of groups, each of which was for certain purposes attached to a particular legion.

Total number of the auxilia. This section should naturally conclude with some statement of the total number of auxilia in the imperial service. Unfortunately, no clear and direct evidence can be obtained on this point either from literary or epigraphical sources. Tacitus, in his survey of the military resources of the Empire in the reign of Tiberius, after enumerating the legions in detail, contents himself with a vague sentence suggesting that the auxiliaries were as numerous as the legionaries and Household Troops. This phrase is perhaps accurate enough for the period to which he is referring, but it is obviously not meant to be precise, and must certainly not be taken to express any principle habitually followed in the composition of the imperial army. If we endeavour to check the statement from other sources we have the remark of Velleius that in 6, at the time of the great Pannonian revolt, the ten legions concentrated under Tiberius's command were accompanied by 70 cohorts and 14 alae. If we allow for a few regiments being *miliariae*, this would represent a little over 50,000 men, a number about equivalent to that of the legionaries. If we may assume a similar ratio in other provinces, the total for the auxilia at this period would amount to 150,000 men. It must be remembered, however, that at this date and throughout the whole pre-Flavian period the government relied upon the troops of the client kingdoms and levies of border militia to supplement the imperial troops. With the gradual elimination of these secondary forces, which has already been described, the number of regular units was proportionately increased. More than twenty regiments were raised in the old king-dom of Thrace after its annexation in 46, and five alae and nineteen cohorts are found in 69 garrisoning the two provinces which had been formed from the kingdom of Mauretania. We need not, then, be surprised if the figures supplied by Tacitus and Josephus show that so early as 69 the number of the auxiliaries considerably exceeds the figure suggested for the end of the reign of Augustus. According to Josephus, Vespasian entered Judaea in 67 with at least 20,000 auxiliaries, which probably represents two-thirds of the total number available in the Eastern provinces. In the Danubian provinces in 69 there were, according to Tacitus, sixteen alae. On the basis of the information given in the diplomata, we can safely reckon that there would be at least three cohorts to every ala, and that one regiment in four would be *miliaria*. Some 40,000 auxiliaries, therefore, must have been stationed in the Danubian provinces at this period. In the same year Vitellius entered Rome with twelve alae and thirty-four cohorts, that is to say some 30,000 men, which represented probably two-thirds of the auxilia in the Rhine armies and Raetia. The garrison of the two Mauretanias, to which allusion has already been made, would amount to about 15,000 men. We thus arrive at the following totals for the auxilia at this period:

The Eastern provinces	.	.	.	30,000 men
The Danubian provinces	.	.	.	40,000
Germany and Raetia.	.	.	.	45,000 ,,
The two Mauretanias	.	.	.	15,000 ,,

130,000 ,,

To this at least another 50,000 men must be added for the auxilia of Britain, Spain, Africa, Noricum, and the small garrisons of the inland provinces, making a grand total of 180,000 men. The next forty years saw the figure mount even higher. The remaining client kingdoms in the East, which were still strong enough to furnish 15,000 men for the Jewish war in 67, were annexed, and the appearance of several new units with the titles *Flavia* or *Ulpia* shows that more than this number of regular auxilia was raised in their place. Even Hadrian seems to have made a few additions to the list, since his foreign policy, though essentially pacific, was based upon a system of frontier defence to which the auxilia were more than ever essential. In Appendix I, where the evidence as to the strength and distribution of the auxilia in the second century is discussed in detail, it is suggested that by the middle of the second century the force may have amounted to some 220,000 men, and that even this figure was probably exceeded sixty years later.

SECTION II.RECRUITING AND DISTRIBUTION

In making a levy for the auxiliary regiments, the imperial government was under no obligation to be at pains to legalize its position. In an ancient state it was assumed, as a matter of course, that the government had the power to call upon every citizen, if need arose, to take his place in the fighting line. Even the privileged *cives Romani* were never freed under the Empire from the legal obligation to military service, however much they may have been spared in practice, so that there can have been little doubt about the position of *peregrini*. Only in the case of the *civitates foederatae* was the government theoretically required to limit its demands to the number of men stipulated in the original *foedus*.

So much for the position in theory; in practice, of course it was not to the interests of the government to raise troops without considering the susceptibilities of its subjects, more particularly since the inhabitants of those districts which would furnish the best soldiers would also prove the most dangerous rebels if the demands made upon them exceeded their endurance. One instance of the conciliatory policy followed by the early Empire has already been noted; the exemption of the Batavians from all burdens but military service flattered their pride and enlisted their clan-spirit effectually on the side of the Romans. Evidence of a similar policy is apparent in the selection of the ethnical titles borne by the majority of the auxiliary regiments. In spite of the obvious convenience of such a step it was unusual for all the auxilia raised in one province to form a single series with a uniform designation. Wherever the clan-spirit existed, the name of the clan was accepted as the official title of the contingent which it furnished to the imperial forces. In Tarraconensis, for example, while the more civilized part of the province was represented by the alae and cohortes Hispanorum, several of the wild tribes of the north and west, such as the Aravaci, Vardulli, and Vascones gave their name to the regiments which they supplied.' The Gallic levies reveal a similar policy; while the contingents of the comparatively peaceful Lugdunensis seem to be covered by the general title of Galli, a list of the levies of Belgica contains the name of almost every tribe in that warlike province. Indeed it is probable that during the first years of the Empire many of these tribal contingents fought, like the Batavians, as allies rather than as subjects of Rome, and knew little of Roman training or discipline.

In the East the historic position of the great city-states of Syria received similar recognition. Among the numerous regiments of archers contributed by this province we can distinguish the contingents of Ascalon, Tyre, Antioch, and Apamea, as well as corps from Chalcis, Damascus, Hemesa, and Samaria, who represented the incorporated armies of the old client states.

The incidence of the levy upon different provinces can best be judged by a statistical table giving the number of regiments raised in each. This is not easy to construct owing to the confusion caused by the duplication of numbering, and the consequent danger of counting the same corps twice over, or of reckoning two corps as one. There were, for example, in Pannonia two cohorts, each bearing the title ' I Alpinorum ', which can fortunately be distinguished from one another because they are both mentioned in the same diploma, but there are scores of similar cases which can only be decided as yet on a balance of probabilities. This extremely inconvenient system seems to be due to two causes. In the first place, when new regiments were raised some time after the original levy they seem to have begun a fresh series instead of being included in the old ones. This process can be followed most clearly in the case of regiments raised after 70, which were distinguished by a title derived from the name of the reigning emperor. Thus we have cohorts I and II Flavia Brittonum, I Ulpia Brittonum, I Aelia Brittonum, and I Aurelia Brittonum. Secondly, it seems probable that when newly-raised regiments were drafted into different provinces they were numbered in a different series in each province. This suggestion is supported by the fact that where a regiment bearing a high number is found, it generally appears that the rest of the series was originally stationed in the same province, whereas isolated cohorts generally have a low number. For example, the greater part of the Gallic levies were originally stationed on the Rhine. Consequently, we find few duplicate numbers and several series which run up to four or even higher. The Thracian regiments, on the other hand, on account of their special utility as archers, were distributed very widely throughout the Empire during the first century, and of the twenty-seven corps known to us, seventeen arc numbered I or II, and are distributed over eight provinces.

Apart from this difficulty the following list contains in any case more regiments than ever existed at any one time. Fresh regiments must have been raised to fill the gaps caused by such disasters as the defeat of Varus and the rebellion of Boudicca, but in only a few cases can we distinguish the earlier from the later levies. It is only possible to put in a separate class those regiments which bear a title derived from the Flavians or later emperors, and were probably raised after 70. Still, if these limitations arc borne in mind, the following table may serve to show approximately the quota which each province contributed:

RECRUITING AREA

	Raised before 70		Raised after 70	
Recruiting area.	Alae.	Cohorts.	Alae.	Cohorts.
Britain	2	10	0	6
Belgica	5	45	1	11
Lugdunensis	2 5	24	0	0
Aquitania	0	7	0	0
Narbonensis .	2	0	0	0
Alpes . . .	1	12	0	0
Raetia	0	18	0	1
Noricum .	1	1	0	0
Pannonia .	5	17	3	1
Dalmatia .	0	7	0	4
Moesia	1	3	1	2
Dacia	0	0	1	6
Thrace	9	20	0	2
Macedonia .	0	3	0	0
Galatia	1	0	0	6
Cilicia . . .	0	3	0	1
Cyprus	0	4	0	0
Crete	0	1	0	0
Cyrenaica .	0	4	0	0
Syria	3	15	1	12
Palestine	2	10	0	0
Arabia	0	0	1	6
Egypt	0	2	0	0
Africa	2	5	3	6
Mauretania	0	0	0	3
Tarraconensis	0	9	0	0
Lusitania	0	9	0	0
Corsica and Sardinia	0	4	0	2

The first point to notice in this list is the smallness of the contingent from the senatorial provinces. So small is it that Mommsen desired to see here evidence of a constitutional principle. The auxilia were ' gewissermassen eine Hausmacht des Kaisers ' and as such raised only in the provinces governed by his *legati*. Such instances as were then known of regiments raised in senatorial provinces were, he thought, susceptible of explanation. The alae Vocontiorum, for instance, represented a *civitas foederata* which was not, strictly speaking, a part of the senatorial province of Narbonensis. It does not, however, seem possible to maintain this theory. The Cohors I Cretum is a certain case of a regiment from a senatorial province, nor can it be really doubted that contingents were also drawn from Cyprus and Cyrene. Indeed, it is difficult to see what legal or political obstacle should prevent Augustus and his successors from utilizing the military material available in the senatorial provinces. Even if Mommsen is right in believing that conscription, as opposed to the enrolment of volunteers, could only take place in a senatorial province with the authority of the Senate (and this theory is questioned by both Gardthausen and Liebenam), there is no reason why levies should not have been made for the auxilia under these conditions when they certainly were made for the legions. In no case did any military power remain in the hands of the Senate, since the recruits would immediately be marched away to garrison imperial provinces. As a matter of fact, the reason for the smallness of the senatorial contingent seems to have been a practical one. Few auxilia were raised from Narbonensis and Baetica, because the greater part of the inhabitants of these provinces had received the franchise and were consequently eligible for service in the legions. Achaia, Asia, and to a certain extent Macedonia, were treated as being on the same footing, partly because Greeks did actually serve in the Eastern legions, partly because of the Philhellenic policy of the imperial government, which would not deny to the Greek states, although they were technically unenfranchised, the privileges enjoyed by the enfranchised urban communities of the West. Also no doubt the Greek of the period was not rated highly as a fighting man. On the other hand, from Cyrenaica, Crete, Cyprus, parts of Macedonia, and Africa useful troops could be and were obtained. The way in which the system worked is shown by the case of Noricum, which, although an imperial province, included many enfranchised communities and contributed recruits to the Rhine legions in the middle of the first century. Its contribution of auxilia in consequence is limited to one ala and one cohort, as against the eighteen regiments furnished by the neighbouring province of Raetia.

In contrast to Narbonensis, it was upon the remaining three Gallic provinces that the levy fell most heavily. From this district came more than a quarter of the auxiliary infantry in the pre-Flavian period and nearly half the cavalry. The Gallic troopers indeed maintained for a century the reputation which they had won under Caesar's command, and Strabo, writing in the reign of Augustus, places them above all other cavalry in the imperial army. Arrian, too, notes their reputation and the number of Celtic words in the cavalry drill-book, although in his day their position had been taken by the Pannonians, already prominent in the campaign of 69. Spain sent the largest contingent after the Gallic provinces, and also contributed a few words to the drill-book, but we hear nothing of the quality of the Spanish troops and they soon lost their early importance. The predominance of the auxilia of Spain and Gaul in the pre-Flavian period is, however, a clear indication of the determination of Augustus to base the Empire on its Western provinces. Archers alone, and these in comparatively small numbers, were drawn from the East, which was still regarded as the home of dangerous and un-Roman ideals.

Lastly, a word must be said about a group of regiments which do not appear in the above lists and are too numerous to be passed over. These are the cohorts which bear the titles *voluntariorum civium Romanorum, ingenuorum c. R., Italica c. R.,* and *campestris.* Collectively these regiments constitute the *cohortes civium Romanorum* to the soldiers of which Augustus left by his will a donative equal to that of the legionaries. From various passages in the literary authorities it appears that they represent the result of two levies made by Augustus in Italy, the first during the Pannonian rising, and the second after the defeat of Varus. When free-born citizens could not be found in sufficient numbers the levy was extended to freedmen. This is corroborated by the evidence of the inscriptions, since the title *ingenuorum* clearly implies the existence of regiments whose members could not make this boast. Originally, as the provisions of the will of Augustus show, these cohorts occupied a peculiar position, and were practically on a level with the legionaries, in consequence of which their commanders bear the title of *tribunus.* The presence, however, of the Cohors VIII Voluntariorum on the Dalmatian diploma of 93 shows that unenfranchised recruits had been accepted even during the pre-Flavian period, and in the following century only their title distinguishes these regiments from the ordinary auxilia.

The evidence hitherto considered has mainly served to illustrate the original distribution of the burden of military service and the respective quotas furnished by the different provinces to the auxilia at the time of their organization. To trace the further workings of this system it is necessary to examine the principles on which the auxiliary regiments were distributed among the military areas and to trace the relations between this distribution and the method of recruiting.

A casual glance at the military diplomata, which give a fair idea of the composition of the more important provincial garrisons between the reign of Vespasian and that of Commodus, suggests that it was the settled policy of the imperial government to destroy the possibility of national cohesion and local sympathies among the regiments raised from their subjects by distributing the contingents of each recruiting district over as wide an area as possible, and making every frontier army corps a mosaic of different nationalities. It will be shown later that this theory, which has been frequently adopted by modern writers, will not stand before a closer scrutiny of the evidence as an explanation of the state of things existing in the second century; it can also be shown that such a principle of distribution was not the original policy inaugurated by Augustus.

Our earliest evidence relates to the composition of the garrison of the Danubian provinces, and the account of the great rising which took place here in the year a.d. 6 by the contemporary observer Velleius makes it clear that the strength of the rebels lay in the training which many had received in the Roman army. His reference to the military knowledge of the leaders and the discipline of the rank and file indicates that regular auxiliary regiments, raised locally and stationed near their homes, had mutinied in sympathy with their fellow tribesmen. Concerning the state of things on the Rhine frontier we have more detailed information which points to the same conclusion. The account in the *Annals* of the campaigns of Germanicus mentions cohorts of Raeti, Vindelici, and Gauls in addition to the *tumultuariae catervae* of the local militia. Later in the century we find an Ala Treverorum engaged in putting down a revolt of their own countrymen in 21, an Ala Canninefatium engaged in the disastrous expedition of L. Apronius against the Frisii in 28, and Vangiones and Nemetes helping to repulse a raid of the Chatti in 50. Finally, when we turn to the narrative contained in the *Histories* of the events of the disastrous year 69, we find abundant evidence that at this date three-fourths of the Rhenish auxilia were drawn from Gaul proper or the Teutonic tribes of Belgica. The only regiments mentioned by Tacitus which are not of local origin are (1) Thracians, who appear on every frontier owing to their special qualifications as archers; (2) Spaniards, who may have entered the province in 43 with Legio IV Macedonica, which was transferred from Spain to the Rhine to replace the troops sent to Britain, and (3) Britons, who probably began to arrive from the newly conquered areas a few years later. Epigraphical evidence adds to the list a few regiments from the Danubian provinces and some corps of oriental archers. In other provinces the same policy can be traced, although the evidence is less abundant. In Africa, for example, the deserter Tacfarinas seems to have served in his own province, and in Palestine we find Samaritan regiments garrisoning Caesarea. On the whole there is sufficient evidence to show that although each of the great frontier armies contained imported elements, in particular the ubiquitous Thracian and oriental archers, the original policy of the imperial government was to draw the auxilia in each case from the nearest recruiting-areas.

Both the advantages and the defects of this system are sufficiently obvious. It saved trouble, a reason which had already commended it to the administrators of the Republic, and it avoided the dangerous and widespread discontent which, as the case of the Thracians shows, would have followed any wholesale attempt to remove the newly organized regiments to distant provinces. Lastly, the men would be fighting on ground which they knew against an enemy with whose methods of fighting they would already be acquainted. On the other hand, there was of course the obvious danger that in a border war which assumed the character of a national struggle the local auxilia might desert to their own countrymen and use the training which they had acquired in the Roman service to increase the strength of the hostile resistance. As a set-off to this danger the Romans reckoned with some justice that tribal enmity was usually stronger than national feeling, and in fact there were many tribal chiefs like Flavus, the brother of Arminius, who were well content with the rewards and distinctions which recompensed their fidelity. Events, however, made it clear that this confidence was misplaced. A time was to come when the border tribes would identify themselves readily with the cause of imperial defence, but the influences which were to bring about this result were often slow in their operation, and the first century saw on almost every frontier a more or less serious outbreak of national feeling, in which the auxilia often participated. Yet even the most serious of these revolts, that of Civilis in 69, showed how the new leaven was working. The political conceptions of the mutineers were borrowed from their conquerors, not from their ancestors, and in the darkest hour of the revolt a Gallic cavalry regiment, the Ala Picentiana, was the first to return to its fidelity.

The first district in which the Augustan policy broke down was the Danubian provinces, and a glance at the names of the regiments stationed here in the pre-Flavian period shows that the lesson of the great rebellion was not thrown away upon the imperial authorities. In Pannonia a diploma of the year 60 shows us the following seven cohorts, I and II Alpinorum, I Asturum et Callaecorum, I and II Hispanorum, I Lusitanorum, and V Lucensium et Callaecorum, forming part of the garrison of the province, and we may add the Ala Aravacorum on the strength of an early inscription. In Dalmatia early inscriptions give the following cohorts:

I Campanorum Voluntariorum civium Romanorum. iii. 8438.

VIII Voluntariorum civium Romanorum. iii. 1742.

III Alpinorum. iii. 8491, 8495, 14632.

I Lucensium. iii. 8486, 8492, 8494, 9834. All these must date before 80, when the regiment appears in Pannonia.

This list might perhaps be lengthened, but it is sufficient for our purpose. It is clear that after the rebellion Augustus imported into the disturbed area a number of regiments from other provinces, particularly from Spain, where the large garrison maintained during the earlier part of his reign could now safely be reduced. The Pannonian and Dalmatian regiments, on the other hand, were transferred elsewhere—several of them, as we have seen, to the Rhine, where they served to replace the troops who shared the fate of the legions of Varus.

The same sequence of events took place on the Rhine in the years 69 and 70. The temporary success of Civilis was largely due to the wholesale defection to his standard of the Gallic and Teutonic regiments then stationed on the Rhine frontier. After the suppression of the rebellion in the summer of 70 a number of these regiments were disbanded or sent elsewhere, and their place was taken by the auxilia who had accompanied the new legions sent into the province by Vespasian. Of the 29 regiments which appear in the Rhine in the second century only ii bear titles indicating a local origin, and some of these had probably not belonged to the pre-Flavian garrison but had only returned to their native country in 70 after a long stay in other provinces. It has been noticed, for example, that of the two veterans of the Cohors I Aquitanorum, to whom the diplomata of 82 (D. xiv) and 90 (D. xxi) were granted, one is a Thracian, the other a Galatian; further, that one of these diplomata was found near the site of the later town of Nicopolis ad Istrum, where the owner had presumably settled after his discharge. This suggests that the regiment had been stationed in Moesia and only returned to its native province in 70 with the Moesian legion VIII Augusta.

It is on these two frontiers, the Rhine and the Danube, that the transfer of troops can most easily be traced, because of the importance of the military events which caused it to take place. In other parts of the Empire other tendencies were at work during the first century which produced the same result in less noticeable fashion. One need only mention the steady drift of troops from the Danube to the East in the reign of Nero, and from the Rhine to the Danube a little later, and it is easily intelligible that the second-century army list shows few traces of the original policy of Augustus.

If, then, it were correct to assume that the title of an auxiliary regiment is always a correct index of its composition, it would certainly be justifiable to comment on the extraordinary mixture of nationalities in the frontier garrisons of the second century. Fortunately, however, the frequent mention of the origin of individual soldiers on diplomata and sepulchral inscriptions gives us the means of checking this assumption and of working upon a surer basis of fact. The following lists give the inscriptions of this type from Pannonia arranged in two groups according to their date, the year 70 being taken as the dividing line; that is to say, the soldiers mentioned in the first group were *enrolled* before that date. Some inscriptions which could not be dated with any certainty have necessarily been omitted, also others where there was reason to believe that the soldier mentioned was enrolled when his regiment was in a different province. To the second group, which illustrates the recruiting system from the Flavian period onwards, a list of similar inscriptions from Dacia has been added. In each case the title of the regiment is followed by the nationality or place of origin of the soldier, stated in the form given on the inscription, and by the name of the province from which he was drawn. For reasons which will appear later the evidence concerning the oriental regiments is omitted.

I. SOLDIERS RECRUITED BEFORE 70 AND STATIONED IN PANNONIA.

Ala II Hispanorum et Aravacorum	Hispanus	Spain	iii.3271
Ala II Hispanorum et	Sueltrius	Narbonensis	iii.3286
Ala II Hispanorum et	Andautonia	Pannonia	iii.3679
Cohors II Hispanorum	CornacasPannonia		D.ci (before 60).
Cohors II Hispanorum	Varcianus	Pannonia	D. ii (60).
Cohors I Lusitanorum	Iasus	Pannonia	D. xvii (85).
Cohors I Montanorum	Bessus	Thrace	D. xiii (80)
Cohors I Montanorum	DalmatiaDalmatiaD. xvi (84)		

II. SOLDIERS RECRUITED AFTER 70.

II. A. PANNONIA SUPERIOR.

Ala I Ulpia Contariorum	Helvetius	Germania	D. xlvii (133).
Ala I Ulpia Contariorum	Bessus Thrace		iii. 4378.
Ala I Ulpia Contariorum	Siscia	Pannonia	iii. 13441.

II. SOLDIERS RECRUITED AFTER 70 (CONTINUED).
II. A. PANNONIA SUPERIOR.

Ala I Hispanorum Aravacorum	Azalus	Pannonia	D. c (150).
Ala Pannoniorum	Apulum	Dacia	iii. 4372.
Ala I Thracum Victrix	Boius	Pannonia	vi. 3308.
Cohors II Alpinorum	Azalus	Pannonia	D. lxv (154).
Cohors I Britannica	Dobunnus	Britain	D. xcviii(105).
Cohors V Lucensium et Callaecorum	Castris	Pannonia	D. lix (138-46).
Cohors V Lucensium et Callaecorum	Azalus	Pannonia	D. lxi (149).
Cohors I Ulpia Pannoniorum	Azalus	Pannonia	D. lx (148).

We may add here a recently discovered inscription from Samaria:
I(ovi) O(ptimo) M(aximo) mil(ites) v[e]xil(larii) coh(or-tium)P(annoniae) sup(erioris) cives Sisc(iani) Varcian(i) et Latobici sacrum fecerunt. *A.E.* 1909. 235. 1910. p. 6.
The vexillation had presumably taken part in suppressing one of the Jewish rebellions in the first half of the second century.

II B. PANNONIA INFERIOR.

Ala I Thracum Veterana Sagittariorum	Eraviscus	Pannonia	D. lxxiv(167).
Cohors I Alpinorum	Eraviscus	Pannonia	D. lxviii(154-60).
Cohors I Thracum	Andautonia	Pannonia	iii. 4316

Ala I Gallorum et Bosporanorum	Bessus	Thrace	D. lxvii (158)
Ala I Hispanorum Campagonum	Dacus	Dacia	vi.3238
Ala I Tungrorum Frontoniana		Thrace	iii. 799
Vexillatio equitum Illyricorum	Sebastopolitanus	Pontus	D. xlvi (129)
Ala I Illyricorum	Dacus	Dacia	vi. 3234
Cohors I Ulpia Brittonum	Britto	Britain	D. lxx (145-61)
Cohors III Campestris	Scupi	Moesia Superior	iii.7289
Cohors I Vindelicorum	Caesarea	Palestine(?)	D. lxvi (157?).

The facts disclosed by these inscriptions are very significant. In the first list, as is natural, we find traces of the troops transferred into Pannonia from other provinces after the great rebellion. It is more important, however, to notice' that before the end of the reign of Tiberius natives of the province were already being accepted for service in these imported regiments. In fact there is nothing here to suggest that any attempt was made to preserve the national character of these Spanish and Alpine corps by obtaining fresh drafts from the districts in which they were originally raised. Those recruits who do not come from Pannonia itself are drawn merely from the neighbouring provinces of Dalmatia and Thrace.

But it would perhaps be misleading to infer from this evidence alone that local recruiting was universally adopted in the first century, although it was certainly common. It is possible that in the Flavian period, when the memory of the rebellion of Civilis was still fresh, some attempt was made to check a national cohesion by combining drafts from different provinces in the same regiment. This at least is suggested by the nationalities of twenty-one soldiers of an auxiliary regiment which are recorded on a sepulchral inscription at Tropaeum Traiani in Moesia Inferior. This monument was erected in memory of men killed in action during one of the Dacian campaigns either of Domitian or Trajan, so that its evidence applies to the recruiting of the Flavian period. Twelve of these men came from the Lower Rhine, two from Lugdunensis, and three from Spain, while Raetia, Noricum, Britain, and Africa supply one each. In Pannonia, too, some Spanish soldiers appear rather mysteriously in an Ala Pannoniorum on two inscriptions which can hardly be later than the beginning of the second century. There are even traces of a similar policy having been pursued in the recruiting for the legions during the same period. In a list of seventy-six soldiers who were apparently enrolled in Legio III Augusta towards the end of the first century, we find men from seven different provinces. In any case, however, no attempt seems to have been made to preserve any connexion between an auxiliary regiment and the tribe from which its title was derived.

When we come to the second century there is no more room for doubt; for all cohorts and alae on the Pan-nonian frontier, leaving out of account, as before, the oriental regiments, local recruiting has become practically universal. Seventy per cent, of the recruits come from the two Pannonian provinces, the majority from the Azali and the Eravisci, tribes which never gave their name to an auxiliary regiment. Even the Thracian regiments, which might have maintained their original character without much difficulty, form no exception to the rule. In Dacia the exceptionally large auxiliary garrison could not be supported entirely by local levies, but the deficiency was mostly made up in the nearest available recruiting-grounds of Moesia and Thrace.

A few examples may be adduced from other provinces to show that the methods employed on the Danube frontier were not exceptional. In Germania Superior three soldiers of the Alae I and II Flaviae Geminae describe themselves as Baetasius, Elvetius, and Secuanus, and the Raetian diploma of the year 107 was granted to a Boian who had served in the Ala I Hispanorum Auriana. In Africa a soldier of the Cohors VII Lusitanorum gives ' castris ' as his place of origin, as do the majority of the veterans discharged during the second century from the African legion III Augusta. Concern-ing the Eastern provinces we have very little evidence, but it may be noted that of the large number of regiments raised by Trajan in this part of the Empire the majority remained stationed in the East throughout the following century, and there is no reason to suppose that they were not kept up by local levies.

The recruiting of the legions during the second century seems to have followed the same lines. The high proportion of men of Legio III Augusta in Africa who give castris ' as their birthplace has already been noted. Similarly of 39 soldiers discharged from Legio II Traiana at Alexandria in94, 22 come from the ' castra ', 8 from the Greek towns in Egypt, and only 9 were not born in the province.' Of 133 soldiers discharged in the following year from Legio VII Claudia stationed at Viminacium, 104 come from Upper or Lower Moesia, and of the remainder all but one come from the Danubian provinces. Further evidence on the recruiting-area of the auxilia dur-ing this period can be obtained from another source, the inscriptions of the Equites Singulares Imperatoris. This corps, which seems to have been raised towards the end of the first century, possibly by Domitian, formed thenceforward a part of the imperial guard, and was stationed at Rome. It was recruited mainly from the same area as the auxiliary alae, and a certain number of the men were selected from them. On a hundred epitaphs of members of this corps who recorded their place of origin, the provinces are represented in the following proportions:

Britain	2	Dalmatia	I
Germania Inferior	14	Thrace	I I
Germania Superior	2	Moesia	4
Belgica	I	Dacia	7

Raetia	10	Syria	4
Noricum .	9	Africa	2
Pannonia .	30	Mauretania	3

The list shows that this *corps d'élite* was not representative of all the cavalry of the Empire; the proportion of orientals is far too low. It was still upon the Western provinces that the emperors of the second century relied, and from these, therefore, that the guard was recruited. As regards these provinces, the composition of the Equites Singulares reflects fairly accurately the relative importance of each as a recruiting-ground for the auxiliary cavalry of this period, and the change which has taken place in the military situation since the days of Augustus is at once apparent. The Galli and Hispani, who were then the flower of the imperial cavalry, and continued to give their names to nearly half the cavalry regiments in the service, have entirely vanished. Speaking generally, in fact, the inland provinces no longer contribute, and the recruiting-areas have contracted to the purely frontier districts. The relative importance of these, too, has altered since the beginning of the first century. The tribes on the Lower Rhine are still well represented, but the contingent of the German provinces is entirely surpassed by that of Pannonia. If we assume that the honour of serving in the Guards was bestowed upon the natives of each province in proportion to the size of the contingent which they supplied to the cavalry of the line, this increased importance of the Pannonians follows naturally upon the universal adoption of local recruiting for the frontier armies ; since not only had the balance of military power now definitely shifted from the Rhine to the Danube, but local conditions required an exceptionally high proportion of mounted men.

The preceding survey of the evidence has purposely omitted that dealing with the oriental regiments, which seemed, on account of its exceptional character, to merit a special discussion. In Pannonia and Dacia we find three such regiments, the Ala I Augusta Ituraeorum and the Cohors I Hemesenorum in Pannonia Inferior, and the Cohors I Augusta Ituraeorum, stationed in Pannonia during the first century, and transferred to Dacia at the time of the creation of the province. Thanks to the recent work of Hungarian archaeologists, the second of these corps, the Cohors I Hemesenorum Miliaria Equitata Civium Romanorum Sagittariorum, to give it its full title, is perhaps better known to us than any other auxiliary regiment. Probably enrolled in the Roman army at the beginning of the second century, at the time of the annexation of the small client kingdom from which its name was derived, this regiment had been transferred to Pannonia by the beginning of the reign of Antoninus Pius, and certainly remained in the province until 240. Throughout this period it seems to have been stationed at Intercisa, where upwards of fifty inscriptions, chiefly sepulchral, have now been discovered, the majority of the latter belonging, as the frequent use of the name Aurelius shows, to the end of the second and the beginning of the third century. Of the five soldiers whose birthplace is mentioned on their tombstones, three came from Hemesa itself, one from Samosata, and one from Arethusa, and the owner of a diploma which dates from between 138 and 146 came from Syria. It is clear, then, that during its whole stay in Pannonia this regiment was not recruited, like the majority of the auxilia, from the neighbouring district, but was constantly in receipt of fresh drafts from the province in which it was originally raised. As further proof of the tenacity with which this connexion was maintained, we find that at the end of the reign of Severus the soldiers dedicated a temple to their *dens patrius* Sol Aelagabalus. An examination of the evidence dealing with the other oriental regiments leads to the same result. Soldiers discharged in 98 and 110 from the Cohors I Augusta Ituraeorum and the Ala of the same name, give Cyrrhus in Syria and Ituraea as their places of origin, and another Ituraean is mentioned on a sepulchral inscription of the latter regiment in Pannonia. Oriental regiments, and in particular oriental archers, appear also on other provinces, and although there is a lack of dated evidence we can hardly doubt that a rule which was maintained along the whole Danube frontier also held good elsewhere.

The reason for the adoption of these exceptional methods in the recruiting of the oriental auxilia was probably the purely military one that good archers were born in Syria, and could not be made elsewhere, but the consequent presence in every frontier army of an oriental element, holding firmly to its own customs and religious beliefs, was a fact of more than military significance. In particular it must be remembered that the enfranchised children of these oriental auxiliaries were qualified and readily accepted for service in the legions. In the inscriptions of the Cohors I Hemesenorum we have abundant evidence of this process, which gave oriental ideas an opportunity for wider penetration.

The British regiments, too, show a tendency to keep up national recruiting, although the evidence on this point is still scanty. In this case the explanation is probably to be found in the intractable nature of the tribes of North Britain, which made it appear undesirable to use the contingents which they supplied near at home. Certainly all the British regiments seem to have been sent abroad, and only one soldier of British origin is found in the province. It would appear, in fact, that the army of Britain was maintained largely by drafts from the Rhine area, but the evidence at present is an insufficient basis for any general conclusions. In Dacia, too, as was natural, the auxilia raised immediately after the conquest were transferred elsewhere. Here, however, there does not seem to have been the same objection to local recruiting for the troops stationed in the province, and the practice was certainly, as has been shown, in force during the second century.

THE NUMERI.

It is clear, then, that in the second century the cohorts and alae of the Augustan system, with certain definite and limited exceptions, were recruited locally from the provinces in which they were stationed, without any general attempt to justify the ethnical titles which they still bore. At the same moment, however, as this principle seems definitely established, there begin to appear on inscriptions certain regiments of a new type which stand outside the prevailing system. These regiments are given the name *numerus*, which does not seem to have had any very precise meaning, and for which it is difficult to find an English equivalent. They also bore tribal titles, a list of which is given below, together with the names of the provinces in which *numeri* of each tribe occur.

Brittones. At least ten *numeri* in Germania Superior. The earliest inscriptions date from the reign of Pius, and the theory is generally accepted that these Brittones were newly conquered tribesmen from the district lying between the two frontier walls, deported after the campaigns of Lollius Urbicus. These *numeri* also bear secondary titles derived from the names of the districts in which they were stationed, e. g. Murrenses, clearly connected with the river Murr.

Germani. Dacia.

Palmyreni. Africa, Dacia, and probably Britain. *Mauri*. Dacia (as a vexillatio from Mauretania Caesariensis). Frequently also in the two Mauretanias.

Raeti Gaesati (i.e. Raetians armed with the *gaesum*, a kind of heavy spear). Britain.

Syri. Dacia, Mauretania, Moesia Inferior, and possibly Britain.

The titles show that these *numeri* are closely connected with the five *nationes*, Cantabri, Gaesati, Palmyreni, Daci, and Brittones, who form part of the army described by Hyginus, and are distinguished from the cohorts and alae of the regular auxilia. In fact the term *numerus* is not invariably found on inscriptions, and for a corps which simply described itself as ' Syri sagittarii ', *natio* may easily have seemed a convenient term. It is also clear from Hyginus that what distinguished the *numeri* from the older formations was their looser organization and more barbarous character, and their titles show that they were drawn from the outermost borders of the Empire, or the most uncivilized districts within it.

Evidence about the character of these troops is scanty; being the least civilized part of the army they were not very prone to indulge in inscriptions. We do not even know the size of a *numerus*, or, indeed, if these regiments had any definite size at all. The *nationes* of Hyginus range from 500 to 900, but the low rank of the *praepositus numeri* below the *praefectus cohortis*, and the smallness of the accommodation arranged for these regiments in German forts, suggest 200 to 300 as a more probable figure. Smaller they can hardly have been, since they are divided into centuries and *turmae*.

As regards recruiting, the Palmyrenes, at any rate, obtained fresh drafts, not from the province in which they were stationed, but from their native home. The numerus Palmyrenorum, which was stationed at El-Kantara in Africa, has left inscriptions covering the whole period from the middle of the second to the middle of the third century, which show clearly what pains were taken to preserve the original character of the regiment. Similar inscriptions of a numerus Palmyrenorum in Dacia give evidence of the same principle. Unfortunately, we cannot tell whether this was the case with all the *numeri*, or whether the Palmyreni occupied in this respect the same peculiar position as the oriental regiments among the regular auxilia.

But whatever the later practice, the original intention of the imperial government in raising this new class of troops seems to be clear. The local recruiting of the regular auxilia presupposes a rapid progress of ' Romanization ' among the provincials and the disappearance of all such national feeling as had caused the mutiny of the German and Pannonian auxilia in the first century. From the military point of view, however, this advance in culture, although it facilitated the raising of recruits, was by no means an unmixed blessing. The old levies of wild tribesmen, schooled by centuries of local warfare, who strove to preserve in the Roman service their local reputation, had qualities which were lacking to the regiments of civilized Latin-speaking provincials, in which national methods of fighting had been replaced by a uniform training and clan feeling by *esprit de corps*. It was to provide a leaven of the old spirit that the *numeri* were raised from the wildest of the border tribes, and not only encouraged to fight after the manner of their fathers, but even permitted to continue the use of their native tongues.

The first experiment of this kind was made by Trajan, when he brought over Lusius Quietus and his *Mauri gentiles* for the Dacian war, but it was probably Hadrian who made the *numeri* a regular part of the military system. It is in his reign that they first appear on inscriptions, and it is to the *numeri* that we must refer the passage in Arrian's *Tactica*, in which the emperor is praised for encouraging his troops to keep up their national methods of fighting, and even their national war-cries. The tribes to whom he refers are Κελτοί (by which Germans are probably meant), Dacians, and Raetians. For the first and third there is epigraphical evidence, and the last two appear also among the *nationes* of Hyginus. It appears, then, that Hadrian was not, as is sometimes stated, the originator of the system of local recruiting; rather he found it already in existence, and sought to correct its defects by utilizing again in the service of the Empire the clan spirit of uncivilized tribes, which had often proved so useful in the past.

THE PRAEFECTI.

The previous discussion of the methods by which the auxilia were recruited has dealt only with the private soldiers, and, as a natural corollary, with such officers as were promoted from the ranks. To the position of *praefectus*, however, the private soldier could not normally aspire, and he attained it, if at all, only under exceptionally favourable circumstances. Normally, the commanding officers of the auxiliary regiments were drawn from an entirely different social stratum to the men, and although the method of their appointment varied and the area from which they were drawn shifted its boundaries at different periods, these changes did not follow the same lines as those which we have been tracing in connexion with the recruiting of the rank and file.

The auxiliary commands are familiar to all students of the Roman Empire from inscriptions of men who went through the equestrian career, the first stage of which was formed by the posts of *praefectus cohortis, tribunus legionis,* and *praefectus alae*. It has, however, been pointed out by von Domaszewski that this system was not established until the middle of the first century. Under Augustus and Tiberius, not only was the relative rank of these posts still undetermined, but they were filled in many cases not by young men beginning the equestrian *cursus*, but by veteran centurions from the legions, especially the *primipili*. We have noticed this system in the army of Caesar, so that here, as elsewhere, Augustus was continuing a republican practice. The following inscriptions, which are both of early date, give typical careers of this character.

    1. C. Pompullius C. f. Hor(atia) prim(us) pil(us), trib(unus) mil(itum), praef(ectus) eq(uitum).

    2. M. Vergilio M. f. Ter(etina) Gallo Lusio prim(o) pil(o) leg(ionis) XI, praef(ecto) coh(ortis) Ubiorum peditum et equitum, donato hastis puris duabus et coronis aureis ab Divo Augusto et Ti: Caesare Augusto, &c.

This system is heartily commended by von Domaszewski, on the ground that the auxilia were thus commanded by more skilful officers, and were more under Roman (i. e. Italian) control than was the case in the second century. The assertion, however, seems far too sweeping, since by no means all the auxiliary regiments were commanded by men of this class ; there were, on the contrary, many *praefecti* at this period who came neither from Italy nor even the more Romanized provinces. The *Histories* of Tacitus show clearly that at the end of the pre-Flavian period a number of auxiliary regiments, particularly those drawn from the more independent border tribes, were commanded by their own chiefs. This practice had not sprung up during the reign of Nero, but was a natural consequence of the development of these corps from contingents supplied by states nominally ' in alliance ' with Rome. The eight Batavian cohorts who play such an important rôle in the rebellion of 69 were so commanded, as well as an ala of the same tribe. Iulius Civilis himself was a *praefectus cohortis,* and two Treveri, Alpinius Montanus and Iulius Classicus, commanded a cohort and ala respectively. All these officers, as their names show, had doubtless received the franchise, but they were employed in their capacity as tribal chiefs, not as Roman citizens, and are to be distinguished from the *praefecti,* who were drawn at this period from the Romanized districts of Spain and from Gallia Narbonensis. It is chiefly as commanders of cohorts that officers of this type appear, since many of the alae dated back, as we have seen, to the period of the civil wars, and had long lost their original character as tribal regiments. This explains the fact that among Italian officers of this period, the title *praefectus alae* or *praefectus equitum* appears far more frequently than *praefectus cohortis,* although the cohorts were of course more numerous than the alae.

During the first half of the first century, therefore, we have a system which differs widely from that revealed by the equestrian *cursus honorum*. The establishment of the equestrian monopoly of the auxiliary commands was, in fact, only completed by a series of reforms carried out during the period which began with the administrative activity of Claudius, and ended with the reorganization of the army by Vespasian after the disastrous Civil War of 69.

The first of these changes was that the *praefecti* ceased to be drawn as before from among the veteran centurions of the legions. Early in the reign of Claudius the post of *praefectus alae* disappeared from the career of the *primipili,* who were promoted henceforward to the tribunate of one of the cohorts of Household Troops at Rome. Centurions of lower rank were still advanced to the command of cohorts both in this and the succeeding periods, but such cases are very rare. A trace of the old connexion between the legionary officers and the *militia equestris* still survives, however, in the regular use of a centurion as *praepositus cohortis*—that is to say, as temporary commander in case of the death or absence of a *praefectus.* The *numeri,* too, were often placed in charge of an ex-centurion bearing this title, an arrangement which was probably called for by the intractable character of these barbarian irregulars.

The employment of tribal chiefs as *praefecti* also became less frequent, as the auxiliary regiments, transferred from one province to another, and recruited from different nationalities, gradually lost their original character. The mutinous officers of the Rhine army, who were doubtless cashiered by Vespasian, were probably the last examples of *praefecti* drawn from this class.

Lastly, the respective rank of the different posts in the *militia equestris* was finally determined; and the order *praefectus cohortis—tribunus legionis—praefectus alae* is hardly ever varied after 70, except that the tribunate of a *cohors miliaria* sometimes appears in the second place.

The result of these changes was that henceforward the auxiliary officers were practically all of one type, men of equestrian rank entering upon what was now the accustomed *cursus honor um* of their class. That this system was not universally adopted at an earlier date is not surprising. The equestrian *praefecti* were young men directly appointed by the emperor, without any previous military training; before the auxilia could be entrusted to their charge a certain advance in civilization and tractability had to be made by the provincials, and the veteran centurions and tribal chiefs of the Augustan system were more fitted to deal with the men who composed the auxiliary levies during the first hundred years of the Empire. As it was, these regiments contained in the second century far fewer representatives of the governing class than the native corps in our own Indian army. With the exception of the *praefectus*, who himself was not necessarily an Italian, the officers—that is, the centurions and decurions—were practically all, as we have seen, promoted from the ranks. But to the Roman Empire, in which rulers and ruled, never separated by any deep racial or religious gulf, were gradually made closer akin by the bond of a common civilization, our rule in India affords in this respect no real parallel.

The majority of these *praefecti* were, at the beginning of this period, of Italian origin, taken from the leading families of the country towns, the class which formed, under the rule of the Flavian emperors who were themselves sprung from it, the backbone of the Roman bureaucracy. The Romanization of the Western provinces led to an increasing proportion of men from the provincial *municipia* being admitted into the imperial service, but until the reign of Marcus the Italian element still predominated. The *praefecti* mentioned on five diplomata from Pannonia Superior and two from Dacia dated 133, 138, 136-46, 148, 149, 157, and 145-61 were natives of Sassina, Bovianum, Faventia, Suessa, Rome, Hispellum, and Picenum.

The accession of Septimius Severus possibly accelerated the speed at which the provincial element was increasing, but there is not, as has been suggested by von Domaszewski, any sign of a violent and wholesale exclusion of Italians from this branch of the service. This point may be illustrated by the following inscriptions of Italian *praefecti*, which can be dated after 193:

VIII 9359. Caesarea. M. Popilius Nepos domo Roma, a *praefectus* of the Ala Gemina Sebastenorum in Mauretania Caesariensis. The inscription honours a procurator who is dated by Cagnat to 201-9.

A. E. 1908. 206. Puteoli. T. Caesius Anthianus, a native of this town, was *praefectus* of the Cohors II Augusta Thracum at the beginning of the third century.

The earliest provincial *praefecti* came from the thoroughly Romanized districts of Spain and Gallia Narbonensis, natives of which appear even in the pre-Flavian period. These were followed in the course of the second century by representatives of nearly all the Western provinces ; Africa in particular sent *praefecti* from its many flourishing towns to almost every frontier during the latter half of the second century, and the accession of the African Septimius Severus at its close possibly gave his fellow countrymen a specially favoured position in the succeeding period.

Only in Britain and Gallia Lugdunensis do the Celtic chiefs seem to have made no attempt to maintain in the second century the military position held by their fathers in the first. It is hardly likely that their absence from the lists of *praefecti* is due to deliberate exclusion on the part of the imperial government. It was more probably a voluntary abstinence, due largely to the fact that these military commands were now regarded merely as an introduction to the civil service, not as a career in them-selves. The Celtic nobles were not uninfluenced by the tendencies of the age. But although they might speak and read Latin with ease, decorate their homes with the material products of Roman civilization, and employ Greek rhetoricians to tutor their children, these country gentlemen living in the midst of their estates preserved a very different outlook to that of the leading townsmen of the municipalities of Africa or even Narbonensis. The Celt retained his martial qualities down to the last days of the Empire in the West, but seems to have found little that was congenial to him in the prospect of forming part of that great administrative machine, in the perfection of which almost every other province in the Empire took its share. The Eastern provinces of the Empire occupy, as usual, a somewhat exceptional position. As in the West, these provinces began to contribute *praefecti* in some numbers towards the end of the first century. A certain C. Julius Demosthenes of Oinoanda went through the 'militia equestris' in the reign of Trajan, and his son, Julius Antonius, followed in his footsteps in the succeeding generation. To a citizen of Caria, L. Aburnius of Alabanda, probably, as his name shows, the descendant of one of the families of veterans settled by Augustus in the south of Asia Minor, the wars of Trajan presented opportunity for a military career of considerable variety and distinction. This officer was successively *praefectus fabrum, tribunus legionis III Augustae, praefectus cohortis III Augustae Thracum equitatae, praefectus cohortis III Thracum Syriacae equitatae, praepositus cohortis I Ulpiae Petraeorum, praepositus annonae* on the Euphrates during the Parthian War, *tribunus legionis VI Ferratae*, during his tenure of which post he was decorated by Trajan, and *praefectus alae I Ulpiae singularium*. These cases are not isolated, and it is clear that a military career was open to the Greeks and the more or less Hellenized orientals who constituted the equestrian class in the Eastern provinces. But while the *praefecti* from the Western provinces were sent indiscriminately to every frontier, the majority of those drawn from the East seem, during the first two centuries, to have been confined to service with the Eastern commands. Aburnius, for example, only left the East once for service with the Legio III Augusta in Africa, and his son's career seems to have been similarly localized. We should perhaps add Moesia Inferior to the list of provinces in which Eastern *praefecti* appear frequently during the second century, since those mentioned on the diplomata for 134 and 138 came from Palmyra and Side respectively. But Moesia Inferior was reckoned in other respects as coming within the Hellenic sphere of influence. These restrictions are probably due to the low estimate which was placed throughout the first two centuries on the military qualities of Greeks and orientals, in spite of the value of the latter as archers. But we may also see evidence of the unbridgeable gulf which still existed between the two halves of the Empire, and of the reluctance of the Hellene to embark upon a career in what he considered to be the barbarous provinces of the West. It is only with the advent of the semi-orientalized dynasty of the Severi that *praefecti* drawn from the Eastern provinces appear in any numbers on the Western frontiers.

In all this the course of events is what one would naturally expect. The spread of uniform culture throughout the Western provinces of the Empire, the prosperity of the ubiquitous municipalities which were its material expression, and the general extension of the franchise which accompanied this development, involved a steady increase in the class qualified and eager for the equestrian career. The admission of these provincial *equites* to the posts for which they were qualified followed automatically without special encouragement from any particular emperor, and the diverse origins of the *praefecti* at the beginning of the third century are one of the best proofs that can be adduced of the prosperity and civilization of the provinces at this period. It is impossible to follow von Domaszewski in concluding from the evidence that at this date the inhabitants of Italy and the more civilized areas in the provinces were deliberately excluded from the *militia equestris*, and that the auxiliary regiments were given into the hands of barbarians. The army was indeed beginning to suffer from the introduction of a barbarian element, but it is not among the officers of the auxilia that this element is most noticeable. The following list of *praefecti*, who can be dated to the first half of the third century, does not bear out the accusation:

vii. 344. Britain. Aemilius Crispinus natus in provincia Africa de Tusdro (dated 242).

viii. 2766. Britain. P. Furius Rusticus. Lambaesis. Severus or later. Britannia Inferior is mentioned.

xiii. 6658. Germania Superior. Sentius Gemellus. Berytus. Date probably 249.

xiii. 7441. Germania Superior. Flavius Antiochanus. Caesarea. Date 91 or 211.

I.G. R. R. i. 10. Raetia. T. Porcius Porcianus. Massilia. 3rd century.

iii. 1193. Dacia. C. Julius Corinthianus. Theveste. *circa* 200.

C. I. Gr. 3497. Dacia. T. Claudius Alfenus. Asia. *circa* 200-210.

These men cannot fairly be called barbarians. Massilia of course speaks for itself, but in Theveste, Thysdrus, and Lambaesis Roman culture vas no new thing at the beginning of the third century. The same may be said of Caesarea, if the capital of Mauretania be meant. Berytus, too, was a colony famous for its Roman character, and Asia was not a province notorious for its barbarism. The increased oriental element, which is certainly noticeable among the auxilia of this period, although not to the same extent as in other branches of the service, is a more significant fact. But however undesirable one may consider the influence of oriental religions and ideals to have been, the conflict cannot be called one between civilization and barbarism. The real matter at issue is the wisdom of the imperial government in utilizing the material which the spread of culture and prosperity provided, and substituting for the old hegemony of Italy a governing class drawn from all parts of the Empire. It is true that this policy was a failure, and that the Empire organized on this basis did not succeed in erecting defences strong enough to resist the external pressure brought to bear upon them in the third and fourth centuries. But if it was a failure it was not necessarily a mistake. It is more than doubtful whether a narrower policy which rigidly maintained the supremacy of the Italians and denied to the majority of the provincials all share in the administration would have been more successful: it is certain that, had the progress of civilization lacked the stimulus which the hope of political power supplied, the after-effects of the Roman Empire in Europe would have been less.

SECTION III. THE USE OF THE AUXILIA FOR WAR AND FRONTIER DEFENCE

A history of the art of war under the Roman Empire has not yet been written, for the simple reason that we do not possess an account by a good military historian of a single campaign between that of Thapsus (46 b.c.) and that of Argentorate (357). Josephus does indeed give a first-hand account of the Jewish war of 66-70, and took some trouble over military details, but his subject limited him to siege operations and street-fighting. The most valuable section in his work is a general sketch of the Roman army and its organization, and a description of the arrangement of troops on the march. Tacitus, on the other hand, who is forced by his subject to describe several campaigns, and remains in consequence our chief authority, cared nothing for the technical side of warfare, and does nothing more than record, as a rule correctly enough, details which he found in his sources.

With strategy we need not concern ourselves, since the subject lies beyond the scope of this essay; but tactics require more consideration on account of the special position assigned to the auxilia in battle formation. From the scanty information given by our authorities it appears that in any regular engagement fought during the first two centuries the legionary infantry were still considered to be the chief arm and employed to deal the decisive blow. They occupied the centre of the line, and the light troops and cavalry—that is to say, the auxilia— were expected to do little more than protect them from a flank attack. This formation was employed at Idistaviso in 16, against Tacfarinas in 18, against Tiridates in 58, against Boudicca in 61, and at the second battle of Bedriacum in 69. It is also prescribed by Arrian in his ' Order of Battle against the Alani. ' The only considerable exception is the battle of Issos in 193, in which the legions on both sides formed the first line and were supported by the archers, who shot over their heads. Dio, however, expressly states that this formation was adopted because these armies were fighting in a narrow space with the sea on one side and mountains on the other, so that there was no need to detach a force to protect their flanks.

There were, however, cases, particularly in warfare against barbarians, where the enemy would not meet the imperial forces in the open field, but took up a defensive position on ground where legionaries could not be employed with success. In these circumstances the auxilia formed the first line and began the attack, and only if they were driven back and pursued by the enemy did the legions come into action. The battle of Mons Graupius, in 84, was conducted on these lines, and similar tactics seem often to have been employed by Trajan in Dacia. In general, however, the auxilia play a very secondary rôle; we do not hear either of the cavalry being used to strike the decisive blow after the manner of Alexander, or of any such combination of archers and heavy infantry as we find in mediaeval warfare.

The subject, however, is still obscure, and it is more satisfactory to turn to the part played by the auxilia in frontier defence, concerning which the archaeological research of the past twenty years has established more certain conclusions. In the frontier policy of the first two centuries we can trace two opposing tendencies at work, each of which is reflected in the disposition of the troops and the duties required of them. At the death of Augustus the Empire had as yet reached hardly any of its natural boundaries, although by means of the system of client kingdoms and ' protected ' tribes it was asserting its claims and intentions in much the same fashion as the powers of modern Europe are doing in Africa to-day. The first century therefore witnessed on almost every frontier a period of expansion of greater or less duration, in which the sphere of direct administration was gradually pushed forward until some physical or political obstacle was reached which necessitated either a halt or a forward policy on a much larger scale. Throughout this period military operations were always imminent; in Britain, for example, between 50 and 85, the garrison marched out almost every spring, either for a campaign or a military demonstration. In winter, therefore, or in times of peace, the frontier armies were so disposed as to be able to take the offensive at a few days' notice. The legions often lay in pairs, while many of the auxiliary regiments, instead of being scattered over a wide area, as was the case later, were concentrated at a few strategic points. The extent to which this system was adopted varied, of course, with local conditions, and a few regiments always occupied more isolated positions, but as a whole the auxilia of a province were far more easily mobilized than later when each regiment had its own *castellum*. On the Rhine frontier Haltern and Hofheim furnish examples of these large *hiberna*, dating from the beginning and the middle of the first century respectively, and we find the same system continued for the defence of the Taunus district annexed by Domitian. There is, indeed, here a chain of forts on the frontier, but they are of small size, with an average area of only i| acres. The bulk of the auxilia lay some way behind the frontier, in forts which held some two or three regiments apiece. In Britain we have traces of a similar system at the same date. The ' Agricolan ' fort at Ban-Hill is a frontier post which would require some two centuries at most for its defence, while the early fort at Newstead, which was probably occupied from about 80 to 100 or later, could accommodate at least 1500 men. The essentially temporary nature of such *hiberna* is emphasized by the character of their defences, which usually consist simply of an earth wall or palisade, little more elaborate in construction than the *vallum* which an army in the field was expected to throw up round its camp after a day's march.

In provinces whence archaeological evidence is not forthcoming, inscriptions indicate the same system. From Spain, for instance, we have an early inscription referring to an officer who held command over four cohorts, and a similar brigade of three cohorts appears at Syene in Egypt in the reign of Trajan. On the Danube frontier von Domaszewski has concluded from the epigraphical evidence that Aquincum and Arrabona each held two alae in the first century.

This period of expansion may be considered to end with Trajan's annexation of Dacia and his failure a few years later to execute a similar forward move on the Eastern frontier. With the accession of Hadrian a new policy begins, which advertised by the elaborate character of its defensive measures that the imperial government was firmly determined to renounce all further schemes of aggression, a determination which was adhered to until the power of decision lay no longer in Roman hands. The outward signs of this new spirit were the abandonment of the old *hiberna*, and the removal of their garrisons to stone forts of a new type, each arranged to hold no more than a single unit, which were placed at more or less regular intervals along the frontier instead of behind it. The auxilia, that is, were transformed from a potential field army into a frontier police.

This policy of passive defence depended, of course, for its success upon the extent to which the frontier could be made defensible. Fortunately by this date it lay for the greater part of its length along positions of great natural strength. The Rhine, Danube, and Euphrates, when guarded by a continuous line of forts and watch-towers, and patrolled by flotillas of guard-boats, formed a serious military obstacle to a raiding force, an obstacle even more dangerous to its retreat than its advance. The desert frontiers of Africa and Arabia were more easily defended, since the routes by which a hostile force could advance were limited in number and the defence could concentrate upon them, and the same of course holds true of the southern frontier of Egypt.

There were, however, districts where such natural obstacles did not exist, as in the case of the trans-Rhenane territory, which was divided between Germania Superior and Raetia, and the northern frontier of Britain, and here Hadrian had recourse to the expedient of erecting artificial barriers, which he hoped would serve the same purpose. In the former case the frontier was defended by a palisade and ditch, which were later supplemented by an earth mound in the German section and replaced by a stone wall in Raetia. On the British frontier, between the Tyne and Solway, the existing remains are those of a stone wall, although there are also traces of a wall of turf, which may have been an earlier work. A turf wall also defended the more advanced line between the Firths of Clyde and Forth, which was occupied between 140 and 180. The southern line in Britain in its most perfect form was guarded by a stone wall seventy-three miles long. This wall was between six and nine feet thick, and probably stood originally about twelve feet high. In front of it, except where the precipitous nature of the ground rendered such an additional defence unnecessary, ran a wide V-shaped ditch. At intervals of about every Roman mile stood a stone block-house, and between every block-house two towers. The mile castles contained barrack accommodation for about fifty men, and reveal abundant traces of continuous occupation. The garrison of about eleven thousand men lay in stone forts of the ' cohort ' size, the majority of which are actually on the line of the wall, although a few, which probably belonged originally to an earlier system of defence, are a short distance behind it. The average interval between the forts is some six miles, so that it was easily possible for each regiment to man the adjacent towers and mile-castles and retain a considerable force at head-quarters. In addition to the troops actually stationed on the line of the wall, there were other regiments in outpost forts to the north and in the forts which guarded the three roads leading south to the legionary fortresses of Chester and York. The ends of the line were also guarded against flank attacks from the sea by forts at South Shields and on the Cumberland coast. If, then, we include all troops within three days' march of the wall, the total force available for its defence probably exceeded twenty thousand men. Taking also into our calculations the natural strength of the position, we may safely say that this was the strongest and best guarded of all the frontier barriers.

The trans-Rhenane frontier, which extends for over three hundred miles from Rheinbrohl on the Rhine to Fining on the Danube, was defended by the same methods, although in certain sections the forts were more widely separated and the garrison was proportionately weaker. There were also fewer troops within call immediately behind the frontier line. Here also, between the cohort forts, stone ' Zwischenkastelle ' and ' Wachttürme ' furnished additional safeguards.

This whole system of frontier defence has been much criticized, and the limitations and possibilities of these artificial barriers must be carefully determined. To take the negative side first, they could not, of course, be defended against unexpected attack, like the walls of a town, unless the assailants were only a small raiding party numbering some twenty or thirty men. On the other hand, in spite of the parallel of the ' Customs Hedge ' in India, it seems unlikely that fiscal considerations played any large part in determining the government on their construction. They doubtless acted, when built, as a check on smuggling, but the expense of their maintenance would have been quite out of proportion to the value of the trade done with the German or British tribes.

The first purpose which they served was to furnish a screen behind which patrols could march in comparative safety, both by day and night, and keep the whole line under constant surveillance. Thus the passing of a hostile force could be instantly reported by messenger or signal to the nearest *castella*, whence detachments could at once start in pursuit. Secondly, whereas the defenders nearly always had a mounted force close at hand drawn cither from the *alae* or the numerous *cohortes equitatae*, the raiders would probably be unmounted, since their start would be lost if they delayed to fill up the ditch and make a gap in the barrier large enough for their horses. This barrier, too, had to be crossed again in retreat, and presented a very serious obstacle to a force encumbered with booty. Indeed, the defenders might reserve the great part of their forces for this moment, as is recommended by Byzantine military writers describing similar conditions.

This sketch of the methods of defence employed applies more particularly to the German and Raetian frontiers. In Britain, more particularly on the southern line, it is probable that a more serious defence was intended. In the first place, the massive stone wall, on which the defenders could stand, was obviously stronger than anything on the trans-Rhenane section. Secondly, we have noted that the garrison was stronger than in Germany, and could be more easily reinforced. Moreover, even after the final abandonment of Scotland, forts were still held in front of the southern line. Netherby on the Esk, and Habitancium (Risingham) and Bremenium (High Rochester) on Dere Street, were occupied by *cohortes miliariae equitatae* well into the third century, and at the last two forts we find a *numerus exploratorum* attached to the regular auxilia. These strong outposts would have been able to check or harass the enemy's advance and give warning to the garrison of the wall of any impending attack.

All these suppositions, however, both as regards Germany and Britain, are based upon the assumption that a raid would be the sole subject of the attacking force, and that it would not be too numerous to be dealt with by the garrisons of three or four *castella*. To a more serious invasion the resistance offered was much less effective. The legions, it is true, still remained in reserve, but they formed the only concentrated force at the disposal of the defending general, for the majority of the auxilia, scattered as they were along the entire length of the frontier, could not be quickly concentrated, and a provincial garrison can rarely have taken the field at anything like its full strength. The system also created serious difficulties when it became necessary to send troops from one province to the aid of another. Three regiments, for example, could not easily be sent from Germany to Pannonia, because each of them constituted an essential link in the chain of frontier defence. It became the practice, therefore, to form out of detachments drawn from several regiments a composite *vexillatio* in which efficiency must have been greatly diminished by lack of *esprit de corps*. A cavalry *vexillatio* of this type commanded by a certain Lollianus, probably during the Parthian war of Trajan, was drawn from no less than five *alae* and fourteen *cohortes equitatae*.

In defence of the system it would probably have been urged that on every frontier the hostile forces were equally dispersed and far less easily concentrated, and that a combination of the Celtic or Teutonic tribes would be heard of long before it was ready for action. The existence of the league which attacked and for a time broke through the Danube frontier in the reign of Marcus was certainly known to the imperial government, and the local governors succeeded in delaying the crisis until the return of the *vexillationes* which had been sent to the eastern frontier, with whose aid they hoped to be able to cope with the situation. Their calculations were upset by the havoc wrought in the army by the plague which these troops brought with them. Even so the danger was eventually surmounted, and the frontiers were on the whole successfully maintained for nearly a century more.

But the full consequences of this system cannot be perceived without some consideration of the changes which it brought about in the conditions of military life and their effect upon the general morale and condition of the troops. A very important point to notice is their immobility. Already in the first century there was, except for the officers, no regular system of transfers, and only an important change in the military situation caused troops to be sent from one province to another. In fact such changes were frequent, and considerable transfers took place, particularly during the Flavian period and the wars of Trajan. From the accession of Hadrian onwards, however, such movements cease almost entirely. During the following hundred and twenty years hardly a legion changed its position and the auxiliary regiments remained almost equally stationary. We can trace regiments which remained literally for centuries in the same province and for the greater part of the time were in the same *castellum*. Of the twenty-one cohorts and alae which are mentioned by the *Notitia Dignitatum* as forming part of the garrison of Britain, fifteen arc shown by the evidence of diplomata to have been in the province long before the end of the reign of Hadrian; and two more, which occur in a diploma of 146, are probably only not mentioned earlier because they were creations of that emperor and had consequently no veterans ready for discharge until after his death. Similarly the Cohors V Lucensium et Callaecorum was in Pannonia at least from 60 to 198, the Cohors I Hemesenorum from 38/46 to 240, and the Ala III Augusta Thracum from48 to 268/71. The best instance, however, is that of the Cohors II Ituraeorum Felix. This regiment is placed by the *Notitia* in Egypt, and other evidence shows it to have been in the province in47, 136, 98, 83, and probably 39. As this section of the *Notitia* seems to date, at the earliest, from the beginning of the fifth century the regiment was probably quartered in the same province for at least three hundred and twenty years. Evidence of continued stay in one *castellum* is naturally more difficult to find, but the way in which the names Ulpius, Aelius, and Aurelius follow one another on a series of inscriptions of the Ala I Ulpia Contariorum from Arrabona in Pannonia Superior suggests that the regiment remained there throughout the second century, and the title Antoniniana shows that it had not moved before the reign of Severus Antoninus. At the fort of Veczel in Dacia the Cohors II Flavia Commagenorum has left inscriptions dating from the reigns of Hadrian, Marcus, Septimius Severus, Severus Alexander, and Philip, which cover practically the whole period during which the province was in existence. In Britain a remarkable series of dedications from Amboglanna (Birdoswald), which has already been referred to, shows that the Cohors I Aelia Dacorum was stationed there from about 211 to 271.

Had the practice of employing a secondary title derived from the name of the reigning emperor commenced before the third century it would probably be easy to prove stays of much longer duration. The figures given above must certainly be taken as a minimum. A second-century auxiliary could thus make himself at home in his quarters in the practical certainty that, with the exception of a few temporary absences as member of a *vexillatio*, he would spend the whole of his twenty-five years of service patrolling the frontier on each side of his *castellum*.

In considering the life which the frontier guards would lead under these conditions we must remember that the character of the auxiliary soldier in the second century had changed considerably since the force was first orga-nized by Augustus. In the early first century enrolment in the Roman service had little effect on the levies of wild tribesmen who composed the greater part of the auxilia at this period. They might be organized in Roman fashion, but the military qualities which they displayed and their whole manner of fighting were inherited from their ancestors. *Promptam ad pericula nee minus cantuum et armorum tumultu trucem* is Tacitus's description of a cohort of Sugambri employed in Thrace in the reign of Tiberius, and in like fashion the German cohorts of Caecina's army shouted their war-songs and rattled their shields beneath the walls of Cremona. In the second century all this was changed: the progress of Romanization had raised the majority of the provincials, even in the frontier districts, to a level of culture which placed them far above their ancestors of three generations back, although they might still seem barbarous to a cultured Greek or Italian. In the conditions of the service there was nothing to prevent the auxilia from participating in this general advance, and the soldiers who spent the best years of their lives in these little frontier stations gathered around them all the amenities of provincial life which would have been found in any country town in the neighbourhood. On the sheltered side of the fort a civil settlement, technically known as the *canabae*, quickly sprang up, and soon contained as many inhabitants as the fort itself, if not more. It was here that the soldiers placed their wives and children, that retired veterans settled near their old comrades, and traders erected their shops. A bath-house or two and a few small shrines, particularly those dedicated to the popular military cults of Mithras, ' the Unconquered Comrade,' and Juppiter Dolichenus satisfied the highest material and spiritual needs. At the fort of the Saalburg, where such a settlement has been carefully explored, an area of something like seventy-five acres was covered with buildings and gardens. Shrines dedicated to the Mater Deum and to Silvanus and Diana have been found, as well as those of Mithras and Juppiter Dolichenus, and two others remain as yet unidentified. On the outskirts, here as elsewhere, lay the cemetery with its inscribed sepulchral monuments, the chief source of our information on so many points of military life. On the British wall no *canabae* have been so carefully explored as those on the German limes, which is the more to be regretted since the buildings are usually in a better state of preservation; but it is still possible to see near the fort at Borcovicium (Housesteads) the terraces on which a scanty crop was raised, while the remains of buildings extend down the hill from the fort at the top to a small Mithraeum in the valley. At Cilurnum an elaborate bath-house was erected for the use of the soldiers of the Ala II Asturum on the banks of the Tyne, and further excavation would doubtless show that it did not stand alone. Where excavations have not taken place the existence of these and other buildings is testified to by inscriptions. At a fort on the Lower Rhine we even find the *praefectus* repairing at his own cost the regimental clock.

The married quarters mentioned above require a few words of explanation. Numerous critics of the Roman army have assumed not only that celibacy is a valuable military ideal, but that it was actually attained until Severus issued his famous edict permitting soldiers to marry while still on active service. Previous to this it is assumed that they had no relations with women but those of the least binding description. Seeck, indeed, has carefully explained that the ' children of the camp ' could not have been reckoned upon as a valuable source for recruits, because the rate of mortality is notoriously higher among illegitimate than legitimate children. This theory is sufficiently refuted by the fact that, as we have seen, nearly fifty per cent, of the recruits for the Legio III Augusta in Africa were giving *castris* as their birthplace long before the reign of Severus. A recently discovered edict of Domitian has shown further that such unions were sufficiently permanent to be officially recognized by the government during a soldier's period of service, although only legalized at his discharge. The effect of Severus's edict was merely to anticipate this act and give legal sanction to existing and perfectly well understood social conditions. Practically the change was probably of small importance, since it seems fairly clear that married quarters were not allowed inside the fort walls after this edict any more than before it, nor were married men allowed to remain permanently outside. Cagnat has shown that the arrangement of the internal buildings of the legionary fortress at Lambaesis, which are proved by epigraphical evidence to have been still existing in the third century, is entirely opposed to such a supposition, and to the general theory, which has often been advanced, that from the time of Severus onwards such a fortress became merely a club-house and exercise ground for the greater part of the troops. These arguments are concerned only with the legionaries, but they are worth introducing because the erroneous views here discussed have often been made to apply to the army as a whole. In the case of the auxilia, indeed, there was never any justification for their acceptance. The evidence of the diplomata was always sufficient to show that even in the first century the auxiliary soldiers, like the legionaries, formed family ties during their period of service which were officially recognized on their discharge. The same picture is given by early sepulchral inscriptions, of which the following, from the Pannonian fort of Teutoburgium, may serve as an example:

' Ti(berio) Cl(audio) Britti f(ilio) Valerio, dec(urioni) alae II Aravacorum, domo Hispano, annor(um) L, stip(endiorum) XXX, et Cl(audiae) Ianuariae coniugi eius et Cl(audiae) Hispanillae filiae vivis ex testamento Flaccus dec(urio) frater et Hispanilla filia heredes faciundum curaverunt.'

This tendency towards matrimony was naturally intensified by the more settled life of the second-century auxiliary. The systematic investigation of the cemetery attached to one of these permanent garrisons reveals as orderly a family life as could be found in any country town of the peaceful inland provinces. The following inscriptions, which are drawn from different parts of the Empire, are but few among many which might be advanced to support this contention.

xiii. 6270. From Borbetomagus in Germania Superior: ' Faustinio Faustino Sennauci Florionis fil(io) mil(iti) coh(ortis) I F(laviae) D(amascenorum), ped(iti) sing(ulari)cos(consularis), Gemellinia Faustina mate(r) et Faustinia Potentina sor(or) her(edes) secundum volumt(atem) testamenti pos(uerunt). Vixit ann(is) [XX]V, decidit in flore iuvent(utis). Faciendum curaverunt.'

iii. 10257. Teutoburgium in Pannonia Inferior:

' M. Ulp(ius) Super dec(urio) alae Praetoriae c(ivium) R(omanorum), ex s(ingulari) c(onsularis), ann(orum) XXXII, stip(endiorum) XVI h(ic) s(itus) e(st). M. Ulp(ius) Similis sesq(uiplicarius) alae I c(ivium) R(omanorum) frater, et Ulpia Siscia soror, fratri pientissimo iuventutiq(ue) eius,' -&c. iii. 10609. From Pannonia Inferior: exact provenance unknown:

' D(is) [M(anibus)] Ael(io)Victorino ann(orum) XXX, stip(endiorum) XIII, dupl(icario) al<a>e I T(hracum) v(eteranorum), et Ael(io) Liciniano an(norum) XII, filis pient(issimis) Ael(ia) Flaviana infelic(issima) mat(er) et sibi v(iva) p(osuit).'

G. R. R. i. 1350. From Talmis in Egypt:

τὸ προσκύνημα Γαίου Ἀ[ννέ]ου ἱππέως χώρτης ά Θηβ(αίων) ἱππικῆς τύρμης Ὀππίου, καὶ Οὐαλεράτος ἰατρον υἱοῦ αὐτον, καὶ Ἀρρίου υἱοῦ αὐτον, καὶ Κασσία[ς], καὶ Οὐαλ[εβί]ας, καὶ Ἐπαφρντος [καὶ] ρᾶτος τοῦ ἵππου [αὐτον].

These examples alone show how far from reality are Seeck's licentious mercenaries and their neglected bastards.

In fact the suggestion of many critics that celibacy is a valuable military ideal, which was attained, at any rate partially, until the relaxation of discipline by Septimius Severus, proceeds upon false lines. In a short service army, like those of modern European states, in which the whole time of the men is necessarily occupied in learning their military duties, such an ideal is practical enough. In the Roman Empire the adoption of a professional army with a service of twenty-five years put it beyond the power of any government to enforce such monastic conditions, and the facts of the situation were, as we have seen, never misunderstood by the imperial authorities.

This is, of course, far from saying that the resulting state of things was all that could be desired. The long service system is, on this account, open to serious objections in principle, and these objections are intensified when we consider the lines on which this system developed. The second-century auxiliary, encouraged by the settled conditions of his service to form matrimonial ties, with his wife and children comfortably settled just outside the fort walls, is perhaps a more satisfactory spectacle from the moral than the military point of view. Military service in the same regiment had not yet become actually hereditary, because the enfranchised son of the auxiliary was advanced a step in the social scale and enabled to take service in the legions. When, however, in 212 the Constitutio Antoniniana swept away a distinction which had long ceased to have any real basis in a difference of race or culture, this obstacle was removed. Two sepulchral inscriptions of the Cohors I Hemesenorum, so often referred to, illustrate this change. The first is erected to a veteran of this cohort and to two sons and a grandson who had taken service in the neighbouring legions I and II Adiutrix, while in the second we find the son of a veteran from the latter legion who has taken service in the auxiliary cohort.

It has already been noticed that the system of frontier defence organized by Hadrian made it difficult either to concentrate rapidly the garrison of a province at one point, or to send reinforcements from one province to another. The more settled the auxiliary regiments became, and the more local ties they formed, the more difficult did it become to order any dislocation of troops on a large scale. In fact when Severus Alexander granted to the frontier garrisons any adjoining territory which had been captured from the enemy, insisting at the same time that their heirs could only inherit it on condition of military service, this act was the natural culmination of a long process of development which had transformed what had once been the finest field army in the world into a rural militia. Unfortunately just as this development was completed and the result stamped with the seal of official approval, the emperors of the third century found themselves faced by new military dangers of a type with which the old system was least fitted to cope.

SECTION IV.ARMS AND ARMOUR

The chief sources of information are the sculptured reliefs on the sepulchral monuments of the soldiers themselves and on the columns of Trajan and Marcus. Excavations have also yielded specimens, very badly damaged in most cases, of the weapons and armour in use at different periods. The literary authorities contain little that is valuable, with the exception of Arrian's description of cavalry uniform and equipment in his own day.

On sepulchral monuments of cavalry soldiers dating from the first century the deceased is usually represented on horseback in the act of spearing a fallen enemy. It may be assumed, therefore, that the armour and weapons represented are those actually used in warfare, in other words that these men are in 'service uniform'. At this period the cavalry uniform consisted of a tunic, breeches reaching a little below the knee, both probably of leather, and the *caligae* or military boots. Over the tunic was worn a leather breastplate with extra shoulder-pieces to guard against a down cut. Metal breastplates 'however, although rare, are not unknown. Scale armour is worn by a trooper of the Ala Longiniana represented on an early Rhenish relief, and also appears on two African reliefs of early date representing equites of the Cohors VI Dalmatarum. The shield is usually an oblong with the longer sides slightly curved, but occasionally an angle in these longer sides transforms it into an elongated hexagon.

This shield was borrowed from the Celtic or Teutonic tribes, as is shown by its frequent appearance on the reliefs in the hands of the fallen barbarian. To judge from these reliefs it measured about one foot by three, and was probably of wood covered with leather.

The helmet, which was of metal, had a projection behind to cover the neck in the manner of the English cavalry helmet of the seventeenth century. It was also furnished with an extra band of metal or a peak in front to protect the forehead and large cheek-pieces which clasped over the chin. On the monument of a trooper of the Ala Noricorum, a very good example of this class, the cheek-pieces are highly ornamented and the top of the helmet is ridged to represent hair. The crest does not appear, probably because it was not worn on active service. It is equally absent from the battle-scenes of the Trajan column, although the ring to which it was fastened is shown. Some fine plumes are, however, represented on the helmet of a standard-bearer of the Ala Petriana on a British relief, which probably dates from the end of the first century. The long broadsword or *spatha*, the characteristic weapon of the auxiliaries, which was probably, like the shield, of Celtic origin, was worn on the right side suspended from the left shoulder by a sword belt *(balteus)*. The hilt ended in a large knob-shaped pommel, and the sheath was often highly ornamented.

The lance with which the soldier strikes his prostrate adversary appears to have had a shaft about six feet long and a broad head. Two more spears often appear on these sepulchral reliefs in the hands of an attendant in the background. These are probably the throwing spears which were carried, according to Josephus, in a quiver on the back, and could not therefore, owing to the position of the rider, be represented in their proper place. Concerning the horses one can say little except that they can hardly have been so small as they are represented. The saddle has a high pommel and cantle and is sometimes covered with a fringed cloth, and the junctures of the harness are ornamented with metal plates (*phalerae*). Like all ancient cavalry the auxiliaries rode without stirrups.

From these reliefs, therefore, we can construct a fairly complete picture of the auxiliary cavalryman of the pre-Flavian period. His equipment as he appears on the column of Trajan is essentially the same, except that he now wears a shirt of chain-mail over his tunic instead of the leather breastplate, and that his shield has changed from an oblong to a narrow oval. It is hardly necessary now to defend the accuracy of the column in matters of detail, but it may be mentioned that there is further testimony for each of these changes.

Chain-mail appears on the Adam Klissi reliefs and is mentioned by Arrian, and the oval shield is shown on a Rhenish relief dating from the end of the first century. The varied scenes represented on the column enable one also to notice further points, such as the manner in which the shield is slung at the side of the saddle when troops are on the march, and the use of the military cloak (*sagum*) which hung down the back and could not there-fore appear on the sepulchral reliefs.

In addition to this service uniform there was, as Arrian's description shows, a sort of parade uniform in which the mail shirts were replaced by brightly coloured tunics, and lighter shields and spears were carried than those used in war. It was with this uniform and on ceremonial occasions that some of the soldiers wore those curious helmets with a mask decorating the face of which several specimens have been found. The fine scale armour which has been found at Newstead and elsewhere probably also formed part of this parade uniform. It is, indeed, always worn by the Praetorians on the Marcus column, but the auxilia still appear in chain-mail as on the column of Trajan. Specially elaborate suits of this armour were, however, worn by the regiments of catafractarii who appear in the army list in the second century. The last change which we can trace was the alteration of the shape of the shield from oval to round, which probably took place in the third century. An *eques* of the Cohors I Thracum is represented on a Danubian sepulchral monument with a shield of this form, and the contemporary reliefs on the arch of Constantine show that it was practically universal a century later.

The equipment described above was worn by the majority of the auxiliary cavalry, but it was by no means universal. The horse archers, if one may judge by a soldier of the Ala I Augusta Ituraeorum represented on a Danubian relief, carried no shield, and possibly no body armour, and wore a leather cap in place of a helmet. Arrian also mentions that some regiments carried a specially heavy spear (κοντός), and devoted themselves to shock tactics. The *numeri*, too, did not adopt the Roman uniform, but kept to their own dress and weapons. The Moors of Lusius Quietus are represented on the column wearing nothing but a short tunic; their weapons consist of a spear and a small round buckler (*cetra*), and they ride their horses without saddle or bridle, guiding them simply by a halter round the neck. The regiments of Sarmatae enrolled by Marcus also presumably wore their national costume, which is perhaps represented in a fragmentary relief in the Chester Museum.

The equipment of the auxiliary infantry in the first century is more difficult to determine. Not only did the soldiers of the cohorts erect fewer sculptured monuments than the cavalry troopers, but on these reliefs the deceased is not represented in the act of fighting, so that we cannot be certain that he appears in full service uniform. One of the best of the early monuments is the tombstone of a soldier of Cohors IV Dalmatarum from the Rhine. The deceased is dressed in a short tunic, which is looped up at the sides so as to hang down in front in a series of folds. The *sagum* covers his shoulders and hangs down his back. A long *spatha* and a short dagger are suspended from two waist-belts (*cingula*) at his right and left side respectively. He has no body armour except a kind of sporran composed of strips of metal which extends from the middle of his belt to the bottom of his tunic. His legs are bare, and he wears no helmet. In his right hand he holds two long spears and in his left an oblong rectangular shield, which is not curved like the legionary *scutum* but flat as a board. On two other reliefs a soldier of the Cohors I Pannoniorum and an archer of the Cohors I Sagittariorum are represented in a similar costume, except that the Pannonian wears the *paenula* instead of the *sagum*, and that the archer carries a bow and arrows in place of the shield and spears.

If these soldiers are fully equipped they have surprisingly little defensive armour, but on other monuments, notably those of a private of the Cohors II Raetorum, and a standard-bearer of the Cohors V Asturum, a leather breastplate appears similar to that worn by the cavalry at this period. On the Trajan column too, the auxiliary infantry are furnished like the cavalry with metal helmet and chain-mail shirt and wear the short tunic and *bracae*. Professor von Domaszewski would like to see in all this a development of the auxiliaries from light into heavy infantry, and it is true that in his account of the German campaigns in the reign of Tiberius, Tacitus emphasizes their character as light-armed troops. But even on the Trajan column they are still lighter armed than the legionaries, and the evidence of the monuments is far from decisive. The tombstones of legionaries of the same period represent them wearing a leather breast-plate, although there is no reason to suppose that the so-called *lorica segmentata* was not yet in use. On the whole it seems safer to fall back on the hypothesis that on some of these monuments the deceased is represented in a parade uniform with which, as in the case of that described by Arrian, the breastplate was not worn. The tunic with its elaborate folds may also form part of this costume, since we know from the cavalry reliefs that the short leather tunics and *bracae* were already in use.

The Trajanic reliefs show several varieties of uniforms in addition to the ordinary type described above. The flying column which the emperor leads down the Danube includes men who wear, instead of the ordinary helmet, an animal's skin arranged over the head and shoulders in the manner usually confined to standard-bearers, and others whose helmets are of a curious Teutonic pattern. These may belong to regular cohorts which had been allowed to retain something of their national costume, but a barbarian who appears in this scene and elsewhere clad only in long loose breeches and a *sagum,* and whose chief weapon is a knotted club, must represent a *numerus.* Others of these irregular regiments are probably represented by the archers clad in long tunics and pointed caps or wearing helmet and shirt of scale armour who appear in one or two scenes. They are certainly to be distinguished from the archers of the *cohortes sagittariorum,* who appear in a uniform which only differs from that of the ordinary auxiliary infantry in the absence of the shield. The most exceptional uniform is that of the slingers, who are dressed simply in tunics with no armour but a shield. Cichorius[5] wishes to recognize in them men from the Balearic Islands, but although the Baleares were employed by the Republic we have no inscriptions of a Cohors Balearum under the Empire. Moreover, if there existed cohorts of slingers with this distinctive uniform we should expect to find *cohortes funditorum* or *libritorum* on the analogy of the *cohortes sagittariorum.* It appears, on the contrary, from a passage in Hadrian's speech to the African army that slinging formed part of the general training of all the auxilia. Like the cavalry, the auxiliary infantry are represented on the Marcus column in a uniform essentially the same as that worn eighty years previously, and no further developments can be traced. The most striking fact which emerges from this inquiry is the general uniformity of the equipment of nine-tenths of the auxiliary regiments in the second century. We learn from casual references in Tacitus that this uniformity had always been the ideal of the Roman War Office, and from the military point of view there was doubtless much to recommend it.

It has, however, more significance if we regard it as one phase in that extension of a uniform material culture through at any rate the western half of the Empire which marks the first and second centuries.

CONCLUSION. THE BREAK-UP OF THE AUGUSTAN SYSTEM

In the preceding pages we have traced the history of the auxilia through the two centuries which followed the death of Augustus. At the end of this period, as at the beginning, the distinction between legions and auxilia still appears as one of the fundamental principles of the military system of the Empire. But during it the growth of certain tendencies, operative not only in the army but through the Empire as a whole, had profoundly altered the original scheme by which levies of uncivilized provincials, drawn from every province, were to support the contingents of the ruling race. Before a century had elapsed the legionaries were no longer Italians nor the auxiliaries barbarians. As a result, among other things, of the steady extension of civic rights, the legionaries were drawn from the provinces, and as a peaceful civilization developed, the recruiting-area for legions and auxilia alike gradually contracted to the frontier districts. Finally, at ι the close of the period, the distinction between *civis* and ʹ *peregrinus* was swept away by the legislation of 212.

From the military point of view also the character of the army had undergone a no less fundamental change. The concentrated striking force of the days of Augustus, which was ready to plunge year after year into the heart of Germany, had been transformed into a frontier guard, scattered over a wide front and accustomed to act permanently on the defensive, every unit of which was fixed immovably, generation after generation, in the same position. This system, exposed, it is only fair to say, to a strain far more severe than its designers had ever contemplated, broke down completely during the course of the third century, and although, after fifty years of anarchy, the Empire rid itself temporarily of internal and external enemies, the military organization was never restored on the old lines. It is our business in this concluding section to trace the stages in this collapse, and to suggest reasons for the change in military policy traceable in the work of Diocletian and his successors.

It has already been noted that the frontier system adopted in the second century had obvious defects.

It can easily be seen that if the strongly guarded frontier line were broken through at any point the internal provinces were exposed to the greatest danger. In themselves they possessed no means of making a stand against an invader. Their garrisons were small, cut down in fact to the minimum quantity required for police duty, and the provincial militia, which we hear of during the first century, seems no longer to have existed except in Mauretania. In fact, now that the army was recruited almost entirely in the frontier provinces, the profession of arms must have been more unfamiliar to the inhabitants of Western Europe and Asia Minor than it has ever been since, and many a citizen of the prosperous little towns of Gaul, Africa, or the Hellenized districts of the East can never have set eyes on the imperial uniform. The situation was clearly a dangerous one, and the lesson of the Marcomannian War must have made it clear that this system could only continue if the frontier troops were supported by a strong and mobile striking force, ready to move at a moment's notice to any threatened point.

In the second century the only available regiments not occupied in frontier defence or police duty consisted of the Household Troops at Rome, i. e. the ten Praetorian cohorts and the Equites Singulares. The Guards were in fact employed by Domitian, Trajan, and Marcus on the Danube frontier, but their numbers were small, their duties were not calculated to increase their military efficiency, and they were rightly looked down upon by the trained veterans of the frontiers. The gravity of the situation was grasped by Septimius Severus, who took advantage of the discredit in which the Praetorians were involved by their support of Didius Julianus to disband the old cohorts, which had been recruited in Italy and the 'civilized' provinces of Noricum, Macedonia, and Spain, and replace them by a *corps d'élite* selected from the legions.

This force, still too small to be effective, was further strengthened by an increase in the number of the Equites Singulares, and the addition of one of Severus's new legions, the Secunda Parthica, which was henceforth stationed at Alba. His successors continued the same policy: under Severus Alexander we find an officer of the Household Troops bearing the title *praepositus equitum itemque peditum iuniorum Maurorum*, a title which implies the existence of at least two regiments of this character, and the *Osroeni sagittarii*, who were among this emperor's following at the time of his murder, were so numerous that they attempted to set up a rival to Maximin and were temporarily disbanded.

Had the construction of a field army on these lines proceeded in time of peace, it would necessarily have involved a reorganization of the whole system to meet the increase in expenditure. As it was, the fifty years of civil war and barbarian invasion which followed the accession of Maximin saw the old order irreparably ruined. The great Illyrian emperors who saved civilization for another century, and spent themselves in marching ceaselessly from province to province, cutting down the hydra heads of revolt and striving to repel the recurring assaults of Goth or Persian, could neither hope to maintain the old frontier lines nor spare time to collect vexillations after the second-century manner when each new danger threatened. Sweeping together Household Troops and fragments of the broken frontier armies and enlisting thousands of barbarian mercenaries, they strove to keep a concentrated force at their disposal which they moved constantly backwards and forwards across the Empire as each internal or external crisis demanded. It was this field army which shared in the imperial triumphs and received such rewards as the exhausted finances could bestow. In comparison with it such units of the old frontier troops, legions and auxilia alike, as maintained their old positions (and we shall see that many did so) sank steadily in prestige and importance. When finally the barbarian fury had temporarily spent its force, and a cessation of internal warfare granted Diocletian and Constantine breathing space in which to reorganize the civil and military administration of the Empire, the provisional reconstruction brought into being by these fifty years of stress and disaster was formally recognized and incorporated in the new order. The distinction between first and second class troops is no longer between legions and auxilia as in the days of Augustus, but between the Palatini and Comitatenses on the one hand, who followed in war the emperor himself and the new heads of the military hierarchy, the *magistri peditum* and *equitum*, and were kept concentrated at strategic points within the Empire in time of peace, and on the other the Limitanei or Ripenses, who formed, under the *duces limitum*, a territorial frontier guard, membership in which was now hereditary in law as well as practice.

At this point we might legitimately take leave of our subject, for although the names of many of the old auxiliary regiments still appear in the fourth and fifth centuries among the Limitanei, there is nothing in either character or status to distinguish them from such of the old legions as had survived in a similar capacity. The title ' auxilia ', on the other hand, is now applied to corps of new creation and barbarian origin which figure on the roll of the field army.

But the very fact that so many-of the old corps still figure on the army list tempts us to consider the circum-stances under which they survived and to take a brief survey of the changed conditions under which they continued their existence. It is fortunate that for the history of the Roman army during the fourth century we possess two authorities of considerable merit, the historian Ammianus Marcellinus and the *Notitia Dignitatum*. Ammianus, himself a soldier, is practically the first historian of the Empire since Josephus to give us a first-hand account of military operations. The *Notitia Dignitatum* purports to give us, what we do not possess for any earlier period, a complete list of the regiments composing the imperial army. It is true that this list appears to be a compilation drawing from evidence of very different dates, but there can be no doubt that it represents for most provinces the general state of things prevailing in the fourth century. The most significant fact which strikes us in these I authorities is the barbaric character of both troops and officers. The majority of the officers mentioned by Ammianus, even those of highest rank, are of Teutonic origin, many being drawn even from the Franks, who are usually reckoned among the more uncivilized of the Empire's assailants. The same picture is presented by the Notitia. Corps which must at any rate have been originally raised from barbarian tribes, who normally dwelt beyond the frontier, abound among the Palatini and Comitatenses, and are to be found in smaller number among the Limitanei. Thus barbarian Atecotti from Caledonia figure as auxilia palatina in the field armies of Illyricum, Italy, and Gaul; cavalry drawn from the Alani appear as a vexillatio palatina in Italy, and Marcomanni as a vexillatio comitatensis among the troops assigned to the comes Africae. Among the troops of the second class we find in the garrison of Egypt Vandals, Iuthungi, and Quadi from the Danube, Franks and Chamavi from the Lower Rhine, Tzanni and Abasgi from the Caucasus, and much the same elements appear in the garrison of Phoenicia. In regard to these troops it may be urged that, since they are organized in cohorts and alae after the old model, they seem to have been incorporated at latest towards the end of the third century, and that such corps, since they can hardly have obtained fresh drafts from their original recruiting-grounds, may have under-gone the same transformation as the regiments of Spaniards and Gauls which were sent to Egypt and Syria in the first century. In the case in question this argument may possibly hold good, but in other parts of the Empire it was no longer necessary to send recruiting agents beyond the borders to find barbarian troops. In recording the presence of a *praefectus Sarmatarum gentilium* in almost every considerable town in North Italy, and of similar officers commanding German *laeti* in all the provinces of Gaul, the *Notitia*³ is but confirming the abundant evidence of other authorities as to the settlement of barbarians within the Empire during the third and fourth centuries.

This wholesale use of barbarians was largely due to the hasty constructive measures which the stress of the third-century invasions demanded. The normal recruiting-grounds of the army were the first to be desolated, and after a costly campaign it was easier to fill the depleted ranks by enlisting barbarian prisoners than to raise and train levies from the unwarlike provinces of the interior. In the same way it seemed statesmanlike to settle other prisoners on the deserted fields, who, secure themselves in their tenure, might aid in repelling their successors. Thus the number of barbarian contingents was constantly increasing, and behind the banners of Aurelian or Probus the Teutonic war-band marched side by side with regiments which could claim a record extending back to the reign of Augustus. The only considerable levies made within the Empire after 250 were carried out in the Illyrian provinces of which most of the emperors were natives, and are represented by the fifty or sixty regiments of Dalmatian cavalry which appear in the *Notitia* stationed in almost every province.

But side by side with the new creations, such as the Felices Honoriani and the Comites Taifali, the names of many of the old corps still figure on the fourth-century army list. The legions had naturally come off best; the most determined barbarian raid seldom took a legionary fortress, and if it did, a detachment serving with the field army would probably survive to keep the name of the corps in existence. It is not surprising, therefore, to find that of the thirty legions which existed before the reign of Severus, twenty-seven still appear in the *Notitia*. From the way in which they are mentioned, however, we can gather many evidences of the storm through which the army had passed. Many detachments, severed from the main body on some special service, were never able to regain it, and are found where the fortunes of war had stranded them. Thus Legio VII Gemina not only appears in its proper place, divided between the field army and the territorial forces of Spain, but is also mentioned as a *Legio Comitatensis* in the field army of the East, and a *Legio Pseudo-comitatensis* in Gaul. The old Dacian legion, XIII Gemina, is represented by several detachments guarding that part of the Danube which was allotted to the new province of Dacia Ripensis, but appears also in Egypt.' Legio II Italica, which had guarded Noricum since the days of Marcus, is included also as a *Legio Comitatensis* in the field army of Africa. The auxiliary regiments naturally did not fare so well. The small detachments drafted off for service in the field army probably soon lost their identity, and the *castella*, which contained the regimental headquarters, must have often been taken and destroyed. Still, as the appendix shows, over fifty regiments survived long enough to be included in the *Notitia*. Naturally the chances of surviving had varied on different frontiers. The section of the *Notitia* which deals with the northern frontier of Britain contains so many names of pre-Diocletianic regiments that it has sometimes been thought to represent the earliest stratum in the whole work. There seems, however, no reason to doubt that the original garrison, although in attenuated numbers, succeeded in maintaining itself until well into the fourth century. We know from archaeological evidence that even the mile-castles were not abandoned until the reign of Constantine. An almost equally large proportion of old regiments is present in the garrison of Cappadocia, which had been spared the full force of the Persian attack. In Egypt, too, most of the old regiments still survive, although they are largely outnumbered by recent formations. The garrison of this important corn-producing province, more essential than ever since the foundation of Constantinople, had evidently been increased to guard against renewed attacks from the Blemmyes on the Upper Nile, who had raided it successfully in the third century. The Rhine frontier, on the other hand, seems to have been swept of its old garrison from end to end. Two of its legions have disappeared, and the other two, which are included in the field army, probably only survive thanks to their names being preserved by detachments which were absent when the fortresses were stormed. It is not until we reach Raetia and the protection of the Upper Danube that any of the old auxiliary regiments appear. On the Middle and Lower Danube, however, the scene of repeated invasions and civil wars during the third century, few of the old troops survived. The struggle was probably a long one: we know from epigraphical evidence that several forts were still holding out towards the end of the century, and excavation may show that many barbarian raids retired without doing any serious damage. But the attack was constantly renewed, and it is not surprising to find that three new cavalry formations have replaced the Cohors Hemesenorum at Intercisa, and that detachments of Equités Dalmatae are now responsible for practically the whole stretch of frontier between Belgrade and Buda-Pesth. Only the Cohors I Thracum C. R. and the Cohors III Alpinorum, the latter of the old Dalmatian army, remain to remind us of the corps which defended this frontier in the second century. On the Lower Danube, where the Goths had crossed in force, and in the oriental provinces which had felt the heavy hand of Persian invader and Palmyrene usurper, we are only greeted by similar survivals. The section dealing with Cyrenaica is lost, so that we know as little of its garrison now as in the previous period. In Africa the frontier had been reorganized in a number of small districts, each under an officer styled *praepositus limitis,* and although we have a list of these districts, we are not told by what troops they were guarded. Only for Tingitana are we given a slightly fuller schedule in which a few old names appear.

The isolation of these remnants of the old imperial army among the flood of Teutonic and other barbarian immigrants shows that the new régime inaugurated by Diocletian was foredoomed to failure. The Empire had trusted to a professional army recruited from a comparatively small section of its inhabitants, and when this army succumbed to the strain of civil war and foreign invasion, and the old recruiting-grounds were wasted, few of the provinces of the interior, which for nearly two centuries had practically ceased to furnish soldiers, held any reserve of military material. By admitting this and calling upon the barbarian to occupy and defend the wasted frontier lands, the civilization of the ancient world showed that it had lost the vitality which might have assimilated these new elements as Gaul, Spaniard, and African had been assimilated in the past. A succession of able rulers and the overpowering prestige of the past kept the framework intact for a century after Diocletian's death. Then when the final catastrophe came, and the Western provinces sank into the Dark Ages, a national revival headed by the still virile races of Asia Minor saved the once despised provinces of the East from being involved in a common ruin. It is with Zeno the Isaurian, not with Diocletian, that the true renascence of the Empire begins.

But the auxiliary regiments which survived into the fourth century need not only suggest to us, by the smallness of their numbers and their isolation among their barbarian comrades, the nearness of the end. The reflection that many of these regiments had held the position assigned to them and preserved a continuous military record for over three hundred years may serve also to remind us of the greatness of the services rendered by the army of the Empire to the cause of civilization.

APPENDIX I

During the course of this essay an attempt was made to estimate roughly the total number of auxiliary troops in existence during the first century, but the evidence for this period was too scanty to permit of discussing further the size and composition of the various provincial garrisons. In the second century, however, the evidence of ' diplomata ' and dated inscriptions becomes relatively copious, and it has seemed possible to draw up something like an ' army list ', giving the names of the regiments stationed in every province during this period so far as they are known. Such a list cannot, of course, make any pretensions to completeness, but it is hoped that the main conclusions which it suggests will not be found incorrect, and that it may be of service to future workers in the same field. The period to which the list is intended to apply extends from the death of Trajan, in 117, to the accession of Marcus, in 161, during which no hostilities on a large scale took place, so that in view of the general character of the military system we may safely assume that few regiments were transferred from one province to another. In drawing up the list the following principles have been observed. In the first place, all regiments have been included which are assigned to a particular province by a ' diploma ' or inscription dated within the limits of the period. Secondly, those regiments are included which can be shown to have existed before and after the period, since they must obviously also have been in existence during it, although their allocation to a particular province is of course not so certain. To this category belong those regiments which, while only mentioned in later inscriptions or the *Notitia Dignitatum,* bear evidence in the titles ' Claudia ', ' Flavia ', ' Ulpia ', or ' Aelia ' that they were created at an earlier date.

These canons have not, however, been rigidly adhered to in every case. In estimating the garrison of Mauretania Caesariensis, for example, where evidence is particularly scanty, it seemed foolish to exclude that afforded by the diploma of 107, the only one yet found in the province. In this and other doubtful cases a summary of the evidence used is appended to the name of the regiment, so that the reader may judge of its value for himself. When the facts seem certain the epigraphical evidence is not cited in full, although to illustrate certain arguments used in the text a reference is given to every ' diploma ' in which each regiment is mentioned and also to the *Notitia Dignitatum.* In calculating the strength of the various provincial garrisons the cohorts and alae are reckoned at 500 or 1,000 men each, the mounted infantry of a *cohors equitata* being estimated at 25 per cent, of the total establishment. For the *numeri,* which probably varied in size, an average strength of 200 men has been taken.

I. BRITAIN.

Diplomata xxix (98), xxxii (103), xxxiv (105), xliii (124), lv (ante38), l vii (146).

Alae.

I Asturum	98 (?), 124, 146. Not. Digit. Occ. xl. 35.
II Asturum	Several inscriptions. Eph. Ep. ix. 1171 dates from c. 180. (Cf. Dio, lxxii. 8). Not. Dign. Occ. xl. 38.
Augusta Gallorum Petriana M. C. R.	98 (?), 124. Not. Dign. Occ. xl. 45.

I. BRITAIN. ALAE (CONTINUED).

Augusta Gallorum Proculeiana

98 (?), ante38, 146.
II Gallorum Sebosiana

103, inscription of the third century (vii. 287).

Picentiana	124
I Qu//ru (? Cugernorum)	124
Sabiniana	vii. 571. Not. Dign. Occ. xl. 37.
Tungrorum	98, 105, 145-80 (vii. 1090).
Hispanorum Vettonum C. R.	103, 197 (vii. 273).
Augusta Vocontiorum	145-80 (vii. 1080).

Cohorts.

I Aquitanorum	124, 158 (Eph. Ep. ix. 1108.)
I Asturum	260 (viii.9047).
II Asturum	105 (?), 124. Not. Dign. Occ. xl. 42.
I Baetasiorum C. R.	103, 124. Not. Dign. Occ. xxviii. 18.
I Batavorum	124.Not. Dign. Occ. xl.39
Bracaraugustanorum	103, 124, 146. Eph.Ep.ix.1277.
Breucorum	which can be dated belongs to the third century, but the cohort doubtless formed part of the early series, which can be traced in several provinces.

vii.458, 1231. Eph. Ep. vii. 1127. The only one of these

I. BRITAIN.   COHORTS (CONTINUED).

I Celtiberorum	105, 146.
I Aelia Classica	146. Not. Dign. Occ. xl. 51.
I Ulpia Traiana Cugernorum C. R.	103, 124.
I Aelia Dacorum M.	146. Not. Dign. Occ. xl. 44.
I Dalmatarum	124.
II Dalmatarum	105 (?). Not. Dign. Occ. xl. 43.
II Dongonum	124.
I Frisiavonum	105, 124. Not. Dign. Occ. xl. 36.
II Gallorum E.	146.
IV Gallorum E.	146. Not. Dign. Occ. xl. 41.
V Gallorum	145-80 (vii. 1083). 222 (Eph. Ep. ix. 1140).
I Nervana Germanorum M.E.	Second - century inscription (vii. 1063, 1066).'
I Hamiorum S.	124, 136-8 (vii. 748).
I Aelia Hispanorum M. E.	222 (vii. 965).
I Hispanorum E.	98, 103, 105, 124, 146. Not. Dign. Occ. xl. 49.
I Lingonum E.	105, c. 142 (vii. 1041).
II Lingonum E.	98, 124. Not. Dign. Occ. xl. 48.
IV Lingonum E.	103, 146. Not. Dign. Occ. xl. 33
I Menapiorum	124.
I Morinorum	103. Not. Dign. Occ. xl. 52.
II Nerviorum	98, 124, 146.
III Nerviorum C. R.	124. Not. Dign. Occ. xl. 53.
VI Nerviorum C. R.	124, 146. Not. Dign. Occ. xl. 56.
II Pannoniorum	105 (?). Still existing in the reign of Hadrian (ix. 1619).
III Pannoniorum	ante 138.

I. BRITAIN.   COHORTS (CONTINUED).

I Sunucorum	124.
I Thracum	117-38 (vii. 275), 193-7 (vii. 273)·
II Thracum E.	103, 145-80 (vii. 1091). Not. Dign. Occ. xl. 50.
Tungrorum M.	103, 124. Not. Dign. xl. 40.
Tungrorum M. E. C. L.'	158. Eph. Ep. ix. 1230.
I Vangionum M. E.	103, 124.
I Fida Vardullorum M.E.C.R.	98, 105, 124, 146.

6,000 cavalry, 2,125 mounted infantry, 20,875· infantry.
Total 29,000.
Legions in the province: II Augusta, VI Victrix, XX Valeria Victrix.

II. GERMANIA INFERIOR.

Diploma 78.   I *Bericht über die Fortschritte der römisch-germanischen Forschung*, p. 99.

Alae.

Afrorum	78. One inscription, which is apparently second century (xiii. 8806).
Noricorum	78, 138-61 (xiii. 8517).
Sulpicia	78, 187 (xiii. 8185).

Cohorts.

I Flavia E.	205 (xiii. 7797), 250 (xiii. 7786).
II Hispanorum P. F. E.	158 (xiii. 7796).
VI Ingenuorum C. R.	xiii. 8315. Still existing in third century. *A.E.* 1911. 107.
XV Voluntariorum C. R.	Early third-century inscriptions (xiii. 8824, 8826)

1,500 cavalry, 250 mounted infantry, 1,750 infantry.
Total 3,500.
Legions in the province: I Minervia, XXX Ulpia Victrix.

III. GERMANIA SUPERIOR.

Diplomata xi (74), xiv (82), xxi (90), xl (116), 1 (134).

Alae.

I Flavia Gemina	74, 82, 90, 116,
Indiana Gallorum	134
Scubulorum	74, 82, 90, 116,

Cohorts.

I Aquitanorum Veterana E.	74, 82, 90, 116, 134
I Aquitanorum Biturigum	74, 90, 116 (?), 134
III Aquitanorum E. C. R.	74, 82, 90, 134
IV Aquitanorum E. C. R.	74, 82, 90, 116, 134
I Asturum E.	82, 90, 134
II Augusta Cyrenaica E.	74, 82, 90, 116, 134
I Flavia Damascenorum M.E.S.	90, 116, 134
III Dalmatarum	90, 116, 134
V Dalmatarum	74, 90, 116, 134
I Germanorum C.R.	82, 116, 134
I Helvetiorum	148 (xiii.6472).
I Ligurum et Hispanorum C.R.	116, 134
II Raetorum C. R.	82, 90, 116, 134
VII Raetorum E.	74, 82, 90, 116, 134
I Sequanorum et Rauracorum E.	191 (xii.6604)
IV Vindelicorum	74, 90, 116 (?), 134
I.C.R.	116, 134
XXIV Voluntariorum C.R.	Inscriptions at Murrhardt on outer limes (xiii.6530-33)
XXX Voluntariorum C.R.	Placed in the province by a late second-century C.H. (iii. 6758).

Numeri.

Brittonum Elantiensium	145-61 (xiii. 6490).
Brittonum Triputiensium	145 (xiii.6317).

Diplomata iii (64), xxxv (107), lxxix (*post* 145), lxiv (153), cxi (162), lxxiii (166).

Alae.

Hispanorum Auriana	107, 166 (?), 153 (iii. 11911).
I Flavia Singularium C. R .P.F.	107, 162 (?), 166.
I Flavia Fidelis M. P. F.	162.
I Flavia Gemelliana	64, 166
II Flavia P. F. M.	153.

Cohorts.

II Aquitanorum E.	162, 166
IX Batavorum M. E.	166. Not. Dign. Occ. xxxv. 24
III Bracaraugustanorum	107, 166
V Bracaraugustanorum	107, 166
I Breucorum E.	107, 166, 138-61 (iii.11930, 11931)
Britannorum	107, post 145, 166. Not. Dign. Occ. xxxc.25
I Flavia Canathenorum M.	162, 166
IV Gallorum	107, 166
I C. R. Ingenuorum	First-century Raetian inscription (v. 3936). Post-Hadrianic CH. (ix. 5362).
VI Lusitanorum	Placed in Raetia by a C. H. which is probably second century (I. *G. R. R.* iii. 56).
VII Lusitanorum	107 (?), 166.

IV. RAETIA.   COHORTS (CONTINUED).

I Raetorum	107, 166.
II Raetorum	107, post 145, 162, 166.
VI Raetorum	Cf. iii. 5202 with Not. Dign. Occ. xxxv. 27.
III Thracum Veterana	107, 145, 166 (secondary title only in last).
III Thracum CR.	107, 166.

3,500 cavalry, 500 mounted infantry, 8,500 infantry.
Total 12,500.
No legion in the province before the end of the reign of Marcus.

V. NORICUM.

Diploma civ (106).

Alae.

I Commagenorum	106. Not. Dign. Occ. xxxiv. 36
I Augusta Thracum	140-4 (iii. 5654).

Cohorts.

I Asturum	106. Several inscriptions (iii. 4839, 5330, 5539. 11508, 11708 ; vi. 3588).
V Breucorum	Inscriptions in Noricum (iii. 5086, 5472). Probably second-century C H. (x. 6102).
I Aelia Brittonum M.	238 (iii. 4812).
I Flavia Brittonum M.	267 (cf. iii. 4811 with 11504).

1,000 cavalry, 3,000 infantry.   Total 4,000. No legion in the province before the end of the reign of Marcus.

VI. PANNONIA SUPERIOR.

Diplomata for the undivided provinces, ci (*ante* 60), ii (60), xiii (80), xvi (84), xvii (85), xxvii (98), xcviii (105).
Diplomata for Pannonia Superior, cv (116), xlvii (133), li (138), lix (138-48), lx (148), lxi (149), c (150), lxv (154).

Alae.

Canninefatium	116, 133, 138, 148, 149, 154.
I Ulpia Contariorum M. C. R.	133, 148, 154.
I Hispanorum Aravacorum	80, 84, 85, 133, 138, 148, 149, 150.
Pannoniorum	Several inscriptions ; iii. 3252, 4372 are certainly second century.
I Thracum Victrix C. R.	133, 138, 148, 149, 154.
III Augusta Thracum S.	148, 149, 150, 154.

Cohorts.

II Alpinorum E.	60, 84, 133, 148, 149, 154.
I Bosporiana	116.
V Lucensium et Callaecorum E.	60, 84, 85, 133, 138-48, 148, 149, 154.
I Ulpia Pannoniorum M.E.	133, 138,8, 149, 154.
I Aelia Sagittariorum M. E.	133 (?), 148, 149.
I Thracum C. R. E.	133, 138, 148, 149, 154. *Not. Dign. Occ.* xxxii. 59.
IV Voluntariorum C. R.	148, 149.
XVIII Voluntariorum C. R.	138, 148, 149, 154.

3,500 cavalry, 875 mounted infantry, 4,125 infantry.
Total 8,500.
Legions in the province: I Adiutrix, X Gemina, XIV Gemina Martia Victrix.

VII.   PANNONIA INFERIOR.

Diplomata xxxix (114), lviii (138-46), c (150), lxviii (14560), lxxiv (167).

Alae.

Augusta C. R.	145-60.
Flavia Augusta Britannica M. C. R.	150, 145-60, 167.

VII. PANNONIA INFERIOR. ALAE (CONTINUED).

I C. R. Veterana	80, 84, 85, 145-60
I Flavia Gaetulorum	114, 145-60 (?)
I Augusta Ituraerorum S.	98, 150, 167
I Thracum Veterana S.	150, 145-60, 167.

Cohorts.

I Alpinorum Peditata	80, 85, 114, 167.
I Alpinorum E.	80, 85, 114, 154-60.
II Asturum et Callaecorum	80, 85, 145-60, 167.
III Batavorum M. E.	138-46, 145-60.
VII Breucorum C. R. E.	85, 167
II Augusta Nervia Pacensis Brittonum M.	114, 145-60
Augusta Dacorum P. F. M. E.	iii. 10255 probably dates from the second century.
I Hemesenorum M.E.C. R.S.	138-46
I Lusitanorum	60, 80, 84, 85, 98, 114, 145-60, 167.
III Lusitanorum E.	
Maurorum M. E.	114, 145-60, 167.

Several inscriptions ; iii. 3545 probably second century
I Montanorum C. R.

80, 84, 85, 98, 114, 167

I Noricorum E.

80, 84, 85, 138-46 (?), 167.

Cohors I Thracum E.

145-60.

Cohors I Augusta Thracum E.

167.

Cohors II Augusta Thracum E.

167.

Cohors I Campanorum Voluntariorum
3,500 cavalry, 1,875 mounted infantry, 9,125 infantry
Total 14,500.
Legion in the province: II Adiutrix.

Third-century inscription (iii. 3237)·

VIII. DALMATIA.

Diploma xxiii (93).
Cohorts.
III Alpinorum E.

93. Numerous inscriptions ; third-century C. H. (A. *E.* 1911. 107); placed by *Not. Dign. Occ.* xxxii. 53 in Pannonia.

I Belgarum E.

Numerous inscriptions, one of 173 (iii. 8484).

VIII Voluntariorum C. R.

93, 197 (iii. 8336).

250 mounted infantry, 1,250 infantry. Total 1,500.

IX. MOESIA SUPERIOR.

Diplomata, ciii (93) *A. E.* 1912. 128 (103).
Alae.
  Claudia Nova

93, 103

  Cohorts.
I Antiochensium

93. 103.

I Cisipadensium

93. 103, 235-8 (iii. 14429).

I Cretum

V Gallorum

93, 103.   Mentioned in a Dacian C. H. (iii. 1163).
93, 103.   Second-century inscription (iii. 14216).

V Hispanorum E.

93, 103.   Inscription probably of second or early third century (viii. 4416).

IV Raetorum

93,03. Existing at time of Marcomannian War (viii. 17900).

I Thracum Syriaca E.

93, 103.   Several inscriptions at Timacum minus (iii. 8261, 8262, 14575, 14579)·

500 cavalry, 250 mounted infantry, 3,250 infantry. Total 4,000.
Legions in the province: IV Flavia, VII Claudia.

X. MOESIA INFERIOR.

Diplomata xiv (82), xxx (99a), xxxi (99b), xxxiii (105), xxxviii (98-114), xlviii (134), cviii (138).

Alae.
Atectorigiana

A second-century inscription places the ala in Moesia Inferior *(Notigia degli Scavi,* 1889. 340). Inscription from Tomi of 222-35 (iii. 6154).

Gallorum Flaviana

99b, 105. Second-century C. H. *(Eph. Ep.* v. 994).

II Hispanorum et Aravacorum

99b, 138

Augusta	Early inscription at Arlec (iii. 12347), which is still a cavalry station with the name Augusta in *Not. Dign. Or.* xlii. 7.
I Vespasiana Dardanorum	99a, 105, 98-114, 134.
Cohorts.	
I Bracaraugustanorum	99b, 98-114, 134.
II Flavia Brittonum E.	99a, 230 (iii. 7473).
II Chalcidenorum	99a, 134.
I Cilicum M.	134.
IV Gallorum	105. Not. Dign. Or. xl.46
II Lucensium	105, 98-114, 199 (iii. 12337)
I Lusitanorum Cyrenaica E.	99a, 105, 138.
II Mattiacorum	99b, 134, 138.

2,500 cavalry, 250 mounted infantry, 4,250 infantry.
Total 7,000.
Legions in the province: I Italica, V Macedonica, XI Claudia.

XI DACIA.

Diplomata, xxxvii (110); for Dacia Superior lxvi (157?), lxvii (158); uncertain lxx (145-61).
Alae.

I Asturum	200 (iii. 1393). Tiles iii. 8074.
I Batavorum M.	158.
Bosporanorum	iii. 1197, 1344, 7888. Tiles 8074
Gallorum et Bosporanorum	158.
Gallorum et Pannoniorum	145-61
I Hispanorum	129
I Hispanorum Campagonum	157, 158
II Pannoniorum	144 (*A. E.* 1906. 112).
Siliana C. R. torquata	iii. 845, 847, 7651.
I Tungrorum Frontoniana	In Pannonia Inferior till 114. In Dacia probably in 145-61, 213 (iii. 795).
Vexillatio equitum Illyricorum	129. (Afterwards became an ala, and is reckoned as such.)
I Alpinorum E.	205 (iii. 1343). Also iii. 1183, and on tiles 1633, 8074.
I Batavorum M.	iii. 839, 13760.
II Flavia Bessorum	129.
I Britannica M. C. R.	110. iii. 7634 is not earlier than Marcus and Verus.
I Brittonum M. E.	In Pannonia in 85. In Dacia in 191 (iii. 1193).

XI. DACIA. COHORTS (CONTINUED)

I Augusta Nervi a Pacensis Brittonum M	145-61
I Ulpia Brittonum M.	145-61
II Brittonum M.C.R.P. F.	In Moesia Superior in 103. Tiles iii. 8074
III Brittonum	In Moesia Superior in 103. Tiles iii. 8074
Campestris C. R.	110. Inscriptions at Drobetae, iii. 14216, 14216
I Flavia Commagenorum	157. Iii. 14216
II Flavia Commagenorum E.	119-38 (iii. 1371).
III Commagenorum	iii. 7221, 13767
I Gallorum Dacica	157.
II Gallorum Macedonica E.	110. Described as Dacia in ii. 3230.
III Gallorum	129.
I Flavia Ulpia Hispanorum M. E. C. R.	110, 145-61
I Hispanorum Veterana	145-61. (Probably is the Cohors I Hispanorum of this diploma.)
II Hispanorum Scutata Cyrenaica E.	145-61
IV Hispanorum E.	138

I Augusta Ituraeorum S.	110. 158
V Lingonum	213 (iii. 7638). But the cohort existed earlier; *A.E.* 1890. 131
II Flavia Numidarum	129.
I Aelia Gaesatorum M.	145-61
I Thracum S.	157, 158
VI Thracum	145-61
I Ubiorum	157.
I Vindelicorum M.	157.

XI. DACIA (CONTINUED).

Numeri.

Burgariorum et veredariorum1	138 (iii. 13795).
Pedites singulares Britannici	110, 157.
Palmyrenorum	Some inscriptions (iii. 907, 14216) are probably as early as this period.

6,000 cavalry, 1,125 mounted infantry, 18,175 infantry.
Total 25,300.
Legion in the province: XIII Gemina.

XII. MACEDONIA.

A new diploma (A. *E*. 1909. 105) shows that the Cohors I Flavia Bessorum was stationed in the province in 120. Total 500 infantry.

XIII. CAPPADOCIA.

No diplomata: the basis of this section is Arrian's ' Order of battle against the Alani ', which gives the state of the garrison at the end of the reign of Hadrian.

Alae.

II Ulpia Auriana	Arrian, 1. Full title, iii. 6743. Not. Dign. Or. xxxviii. 23.
I Augusta Gemina Colonorum	Arrian, 1. Full title, viii. 8934. Not. Dign. Or. xxxviii. 21.
II Gallorum	Arrian, 9. Cf. I. G. R. R. iii. 272 ; Not. Dign. Or. xxxviii. 24.
I Ulpia Dacorum	Arrian, 8. Not. Dign. Or. xxxviii. 23.

Cohorts.

Apuleia C. R.	Arrian, 7 and 14. Not. Dign. Or. xxxviii. 34.

XIII. CAPPADOCIA. COHORTS (CONTINUED).

Bosporiana M. S.	Arrian, 3 and 18. Not. Dign. Or. xxxviii. 29
I Claudia E.	Not. Dign. Or. xxxviii. 36.
Cyrenaica S. E.	Arrian, 1 and 14.
I Germanorum M.	Arrian, 2. Cf. I. G. R. R. i. 623 ; Not. Dign. Or. xxxviii. 30.
II Hispanorum	E. Cf. iii. 6760, ix. 2649; *A . E .* 1911. 161.
II Italica C. R. S. M. E.	Arrian, 3, 9, and 13. Cf. xi. 6117.

Ituraeorum E.	Arrian, I
I Lepidiana E. C. R.	In Moesia Inferior in 98-114. Not. Dign. Or. xxxviii. 35.
I Flavia Numidarum M. E. S.	Arrian,3 and 18. Cf. D. lxxvi (178) for Lycia-Pamphylia.
III Ulpia Petraeorum	Arrian, I. Not. Dign. Or. xxxviii. 27.
I Raetorum E.	Arrian, I.
IV Raetorum E.	Arrian, I.

2,000 cavalry, 1,875 mounted infantry, 7,5 infantry.
Total 11,000.
Legions in the province: XII Fulminata, XV Apollinaris.

XIV. SYRIA.

Diploma cx (157). The cavalry vexillatio described in iii. 600 seems to have been drawn almost entirely from regiments stationed in the Eastern provinces. This inscription, therefore, Which probably dates from the end of Trajan's reign, may be reckoned as a diploma, and the regiments mentioned in it placed in Syria if they cannot be traced elsewhere.

Alae.

II Flavia Agrippiana	iii. 600. Cf. C. I. G. iii. 3497 for full titles.
Augusta Syriaca	iii. 600 (from Egypt).
I Ulpia Dromedariorum M.	157.
I Praetoria C. R.	iii. 600. Not. Dign. Or. xxxviii. 26 (in Armenia).
III Thracum	Cf. ii. 4251 (praefectus alae III Thracum in Syria) with vi. 1449, which shows that the regiment was existing in the middle of the second century.
Thracum Herculania M.	iii. 600, 157
I Ulpia Singularium	iii. 600, 157

Cohorts.

I Ascalonitanorum S. E.	iii. 600, 157.
I Flavia Chalcidenorum S. E.	157.
V Chalcidenorum E.	iii. 600
II Classica S.	157.
I Ulpia Dacorum	157. Not. Dign. Or. xxxiii. 33 (Syria)
III Dacorum E.	iii. 600.
II Equitum	iii. 600.
VII Gallorum	157.
I Lucensium E.	iii. 600 (from Dalmatia).
IV Lucensium E.	iii. 600
II Ulpia Paflagonum E.	iii. 600. 157

XIV. SYRIA.   COHORTS (CONTINUED).

III Ulpia Paflagonum E.	iii. 600, 157.
I Ulpia Petraeorum M. E.	iii. 600, 157.
V Ulpia Petraeorum M.E.	iii. 600, 157.
I Ulpia Sagittariorum E.	iii. 600.
I Claudia Sugambrorum	157.
I Sugambrorum E.	iii. 600 (from Moesia).
II Thracum Syriaca E.	157.
III Augusta Thracum E.	157.

III Thracum Syriaca E.	*A. E.* 1911. 161.
IV Thracum Syriaca E.	Mentioned on a C. H. of the second century (ii. 1970).
II Ulpia E. C. R. iii. 600, 157.	

4,500 cavalry, 2,75 mounted infantry, 9,625 infantry.
Total 16,500.
Legions in the province: III Gallica, IV Scythica, XVI Flavia.

XV. SYRIA PALAESTINA.

Diplomata, xix (86), cix (139).
Alae.

Gallorum et Thracum	139.
Anton. . . . Gallorum	139. Probably the εἴλη Ἀντωνινιανὴ Γαλικὴ of *B. G. U.* 614 (dated 217).
VII Phrygum	139.
Cohorts.	
III Bracarum	139.
IV Breucorum	139.
I Damascenorum	139.

XV. SYRIA PALAESTINA COHORTS (CONTINUED)

I Flavia C. R. E.	iii. 600, 139. Not. Dign. Or. xxxiv. 45.
I Ulpia Galatarum	139.
II Ulpia Galatarum	139. Not. Dign. Or. xxxiv. 44.
V Gemina C. R.	139.
I Montanorum	139.
IV Ulpia Petraeorum	139.
VI Ulpia Petraeorum	139.
I Sebastenorum M.	139.
I Thracum M	139. Not. Dign. Or. xxxvii. 31 (Arabia).

1,500 cavalry, 125 mounted infantry, 6,875 infantry.
Total 8,500.
Legions in the province: VI Ferrata, X Fretensis.

XVI. ARABIA.

Auxilia as yet unknown. Legio III Cyrenaica was stationed in the province.

XVII. EGYPT.

Diploma xv (83).
Alae.

Apriana	83, 170 (iii. 49) Not. Dign. Or. xxviii. 32.
II Ulpia Afrorum	Not. Dign. Or. xxviii. 38
Gallorum Veterana	199 (iii. 6581). Unlikely to be a late creation. Not. Dign. Or. xxviii. 28.
I Thracum Mauretana	154-5 (B.C. U. 447), 156 (Eph. Ep. vii. p. 457).

Vocontiorum   134 (B. G. U. 114).

Cohorts.
I Ulpia Afrorum E.   177 (B. G. U. 241).

I Apamenorum S. E.   145 (Brit.Mus.Pap.178).

XVII. EGYPT. COHORTS (CONTINUED).

I Flavia Cilicum E   140 (iii. 6025).

III Cilicum   217-18 (A. E. 1905. 54), but it belonged presumably to
                                                   the early series

                                                   Not. Dign. Or. xxviii. 35, but belonging probably to the
                                                   series raised by Trajan.
III Galatarum

II Hispanorum   134 (B.G. U. 114).

II Ituraeorum Felix E.   147 (I. G. R. R. i. 1348). Not. Dign. Or. xxviii. 44.

III Ituraeorum   103 (Pap. Ox. vii. 1022). A second-century C. H. (viii.
                                                   17904).

I Augusta Praetoria Lusitanorum   E. 156 (Eph. Ep. vii. p. 456). Not. Dign. Or. xxxi. 58
I Augusta Pannoniorum   83. Not. Dign. Or. xxviii. 41.
Scutata C. R.   143 (B. G. U. 141).   Cf. iii. 12069 and Not. Dign. Or.
                                                   xxxi. 59.
I Thebaeorum E.   114 (B.G. U. 114).
II Thracum   167 (Wilcken, Ostraka, 927).

Numeri.
Palmyreni Hadriani Sagittarii   216 (I.G.R.R. i. 1169).
2,500 cavalry, 750 mounted infantry, 5,950 infantry.
Total 9,200.
Legion in the province: II Traiana Fortis.

XVIII. CYRENAICA.

Garrison unknown.

XIX. AFRICA

Alae.

Flavia   174 (viii. 21567).
I Augusta Pannoniorum   128. Addressed by Hadrian (*A . E.* 1900. 33).
Cohorts.
II Flavia Afrorum   198 (*A. E.* 1909. 104).

I Chalcidenorum E.   164 (viii. 17587).

VI Commagenorum E.

                                                   128. Addressed by Hadrian (viii. 18042).

XIX. AFRICA. COHORTS (CONTINUED).

I Flavia E.
II Hispanorum E.
II Maurorum
Numeri.
Palmyrenorum
1, 000 cavalry, 500 mounted infantry, 2,700 infantry.
Total 4,200.
Legion in the province: III Augusta.

128. Addressed by Hadrian (viii. 18042).
128. Addressed by Hadrian (viii. 18042).
208 (viii. 4323).

211-17 (viii. 18007).

XX. MAURETANIA CAESARIENSIS

Diploma xxxvi (107).
Alae.

Brittonum V.

Second - century inscription (viii. 9764). Cf. 593

Miliaria

Several inscriptions (viii. 9389, 21029, 21036, 21568, 21618). Existed in second century (xii. 672). 107.

I Nerviana Augusta Fidelis M.
I Augusta Parthorum

107
107, 201 (viii. 9827).

Flavia Gemina Sebastenorum

234 (viii. 21039). A *praefectus* of the reign of Marcus (*Eph. Ep.* 699).

II Augusta Thracum P.F.
Cohorts.
II Breucorum E.

107, 209-11 (viii. 9370).

107, 243 (viii. 21560). 107.

II Brittonum
I Corsorum C. R.

107
Post-Hadrianic C. H. (ix. 2853).

II Gallorum
I Flavia Hispanorum
I Flavia Musulamiorum
I Augusta Nerviana Velox
I Nurritanorum

107
107, 201 (viii. 9360)
107
107
Later inscriptions (xi. 6010 ; viii. 4292).

XX. MAURETANIA CAESARIENSIS. COHORTS (CONTINUED).

I Pannoniorum E.

107, 201 (viii. 22602).

II Sardorum

208 (viii. 21721). Also first-century inscriptions.

I Aelia Singularium

260 (viii. 9047). Cf. 20753.

IV Sugambrorum

107, 255 (viii. 9045).

Numeri.
Gaesatorum

150 (viii. 2728).

4,000 cavalry, 250 mounted infantry, 5,950 infantry.
Total 10,00.
Third-century inscriptions also show the existence of a large force of Moorish irregular cavalry, perhaps a sort of territorial militia. It is impossible, however, to estimate their number, or to ascertain whether they were already in existence in the second century. Cf. Cagnat, *L'armée romaine d'Afrique*, pp. 261-73.

XXI. MAURETANIA TINGITANA.

Alae.
Hamiorum

A second-century inscription (viii. 21814a). Cf. *A . E .* 1906. 119

Cohorts.
I Asturum et Callaecorum M.

C. H. of reign of Trajan (ii. 4211). Cf. viii. 21820; vi. 3654.

III Asturum C. R. E.

Late second-century C. H. (xi. 4371). Placed in Mauretania by a Greek inscription (Waddington, 104) and Not. Dign. Occ. xx vi. 19.

500 cavalry, 125 mounted infantry, 1,375 infantry. Total 2,000.

XXII. HISPANIA TARRACONENSIS

Alae.
II Flavia Hispanorum
I Lemavorum

CR. 184 (cf. *A . E .* 1910. 5 ; ii. 2600).
161-7 or later (ii. 2103).

XXII. HISPANIA TARRACONENSIS (CONTINUED).

Cohorts.
I Celtiberorum Baetica E.
III Celtiberorum
I Gallica E.
II Gallica

163 (ii. 2552 ; cf. A. E. 1910. 3).
167 (A. E. 1910. 4).
A.E. 1910. 4. Not. Dign. Occ. xiii. 32
Not. Dign. Occ. xlii. 28. It is stationed at 'Cohors Gallica'.

III Lucensium

Inscriptions ii. 2584, 4132. Cf. Not. Dign. Occ. xiii. 29.

1,000 cavalry, 250 mounted infantry, 2,250 infantry.
Total 3,500.
Legion in the province: VII Gemina.
To this list we may add the following regiments, which can be shown to have existed in the second century, although they cannot be assigned to any particular province:

Alae.
III Asturum
I Flavia Gallorum Tauriana

xi. 3007 (the name Ulpius occurs).
viii. 2394, 2395 (Trajan at earliest).

Cohorts.
Aelia Expedita
II Bracarum
III Breucorum

viii. 9358.
vi. 1838 (Trajan)
ix. 4753 (Trajan); x. 3847 (probably middle of second century).

VI Brittonum
III Augusta Cyrenaica

ii. 2424 (Trajan).
Römische Mitteilungen, iii. 77 (Marcus).

VI Gallorum

vi. 1449. The career of the Praefectus Praetorio Macrinius Vindex, who was killed in72. He probably commanded this cohort about 150.

VI Hispanorum	xi. 4376 (Trajan).
III Lingonum E.	xi. 5959 (Trajan or later).
Pannoniorumet Dalmatarum	χ. 5829 (Trajan).
II Ulpia Petraeorum M. E.	xi. 5669 (Trajan or Hadrian).
V Raetorum	viii. 8934 (Trajan to Hadrian).
1,000 cavalry, 375 mounted infantry, 5, 125 infantry.	
Total 6,500.	

These calculations show that during the period in question the auxiliary troops amounted to 47,500 cavalry, 15,75 mounted infantry, and 129,925 infantry, giving a total establishment of 191,800 men. It is probable, however, that this puts the proportion of mounted men too low. Arrian's *Ectaxis* shows that nearly every cohort of the Cappadocian garrison was *equitata,* and although the proportion of mounted men was doubtless higher on the eastern frontier than on the Rhine or in Britain, it is probable that if we possessed more documents similar to the *Ectaxis* dealing with the other garrisons we should find a higher proportion of *cohortes equitatae* than our present evidence suggests. It is equally probable that the total figure arrived at falls below the reality. For no province is it likely that the list is complete; in some cases, such as Mauretania Tingitana and Africa, the garrison is obviously put far below its real establishment, while for Arabia and Cyrenaica we have no evidence at all. The deficiency is certainly too great to be made good by the few regiments of uncertain habitation which conclude the list. Probably we may reckon on a total figure of about 220,000 men, of whom at least 80,000 would be mounted. The twenty-eight legions in existence at this time, if we follow Suetonius in assigning 5,600 men to a legion, would only have a total establishment of 156,800, so that clearly in dealing with the army at this period we must disregard Tacitus's statement that the auxilia were approximately equal in number to the legionaries.

The total military establishment of the Empire at the accession of Marcus including the Household Troops, that is to say the ten Praetorian and six Urban cohorts and the Equités Singulares, and the complement of the fleets in the Mediterranean and the Channel and on the Rhine, Danube, and Euphrates, must thus have amounted to some 420,000 men. This total, however, was to be still further increased before the decline began. At the beginning of the third century when additions had been made to the Household Troops, when the legions had been increased to thirty-three[1] and scores of *numeri* added to the frontier guards, there may have been nearly half a million men serving with the colours, a larger disciplined force than was at the disposal of any one state before the nineteenth century, and the largest professional army which the world has ever seen.

APPENDIX II

Tʜɪs appendix is mainly designed to supplement the table on p. 60, by giving a list of the auxiliary regiments grouped according to the provinces in which they were raised. I have also added for the sake of completeness a further section dealing with the *cohortes civium Romanorum,* and a few regiments of which we do not know the place of origin. The list thus contains, or is intended to contain, the names of all the auxiliary regiments known to us, and includes far more than existed at any one time. The greater part of this list is, of course, merely a repetition of that drawn up by Cichorius in his articles on *ala* and *cohors* contributed to Pauly-Wissowa, and in view of the admirable summary of the evidence there given I have restricted myself to appending to the title of each regiment the name of the province in which it was stationed, or, when this is unknown, a reference to a single inscription mentioning it. Only in cases where I have been able to add to the list a regiment unknown when Cichorius wrote have I added a note on the evidence. The whole may, in fact, be described as a summary of Cichorius's articles, with a supplement bringing them up to date, and as such may, I hope, be of some value to students of this subject.

As in the list on p. 60, regiments raised before 70 and those of later date are divided into two groups, distinguished by the letters A and B.

BRITAIN

Alae
A. I Flavia Augusta Britannica M. C. R.	Germania Superior—Pannonia Inferior.
Brittonum V.	Mauretania Caesariensis.
A. I Britannica M. C. R.	Pannonia— Dacia
I Brittonum M. E.	Pannonia—Dacia

II Brittonum M. C. R. P. F.	Dacia
II Brittonum	Mauretania Caesariensis
III Brittannorum	Raetia
III Brittonum	Dacia
III Brittonum V. E.	xi. 393
IV and V Brittonum supposed because of the existence of	
VI Brittonum	ii. 2424

B. I Flavia Brittonum	Dalmatia—Noricum.
I Ulpia Brittonum M.	Dacia
I Aelia Brittonum M.	Noricum
I Augusta Nervia Pacensis Brittonum M.	Dacia
I Aurelia Brittonum M.	Dacia
II Flavia Brittonum	Moesia Inferior.
II Augusta Nervia Pacensis Brittonum M.	Pannonia Inferior.

BELGICA.

Alae.

A. Batavorum	Germania Inferior.
I Canninefatium C.R.	Germania Superior—Pannonia Superior.
Treverorum	Germania Inferior
Tungrorum Frontoniana	Dalmatia—Pannonia—Dacia
I Tungrorum	Britain
B. I Batavorum M.	Dacia

Cohorts.

A. I Batavorum C. R.	Britain
I-VIII Batavorum M.	The regiments which joined the rebellion of Civilis and were presumably disbanded.
IX Batavorum M. E.	Raetia.
I Belgarum E.	Dalmatia.

BELGICA.

Cohorts (continued).

I Belgica	Germania Superior
Cohortes Canninefatium	Joined the rebellion of Civilis and were presumably disbanded in consequence. Cf. Tac. Hist. iv.19
I Frisiavonum	Britain
I Germanorum C. R.	Germania Superior
I Germanorum M. E.	Cappadocia
I Lingonum E.	Britain
II Lingonum E.	Britain
III Lingonum E.	xi.5959
IV Lingonum E.	Britain
V Lingonum E.	Dacia
I Menapiorum	Britain
I Menapiorum	Britain
Nemetum	Germania Superior
I Nerviorum	Britain
II Nerviorum	Britain
III Nerviorum C.R.	Britain
IV and V Nerviorum C. R. supposed on account of the existence of	
VI Nerviorum C. R.	Britain.
I Sequanorum et Rauracorum E.	Germania Superior

I Sugambrorum V. E.	Moesia Inferior—Syria.
I Claudia Sugambrorum	Moesia Inferior—Syria
II and III Sugambrorum supposed on account of the existence of	
IV Sugambrorum	Mauretania Caesariensis
I Sunucorum	Britain
I Tungrorum M.	Germania Inferior—Britain.
II Tungrorum M. E. C. L.	Germania Inferior—Britain
Cohortes Ubiorum	Germania Inferior, cf. Tac. Hist. iv. 28
I Ubiorum	Moesia Inferior—Dacia.
Usiporum	Tac.Agr.28
I Vangionum M. E.	Germania Inferior—Britain.
B. I Batavorum M.	Pannonia—Dacia
I Batavorum	Britain
III Batavorum M.	Pannonia

BELGICA.

Cohorts (continued).

III Batavorum M.	Pannonia Inferior.
I Septimia Belgarum	Germania Superior.
I Ulpia Traiana Cugernorum	Britain.
I Nervana Germanorum M. Britain.	
I Mattiacorum supposed on account of the existence of	
II Mattiacorum	Moesia Inferior.
I Treverorum supposed on account of the existence of	
II Treverorum	Germania Superior.

LUGDUNENSIS
Alae.

A. Gallorum Flaviana	Moesia Inferior
Gallorum Indiana	Germania Inferior—Britain—Germania Superior.
Augusta Gallorum Petriana M.	Germania Superior—Britain
Augusta Gallorum Proculeiana	Britain
Gallorum V	Egypt
I Flavia Gallorum Tauriana	Gaul
I Claudia Gallorum	Moesia Inferior
I Gallorum et Bosporanorum	Dacia
I Gallorum et Pannoniorum	Moesia Inferior
II Gallorum Sebosiana	Germania Superior—Britain
II Gallorum	Cappadocia

The majority of the following regiments, which bear titles derived from personal names, can be shown to have received recruits from the Gallic provinces, where it is probable that all were originally raised.

Agrippiana	Germania Superior—Britain.
II Flavia Agrippiana	Syria.

LUGDUNENSIS.

Alae(continued)

Apriana	Egypt
Atectorigiana	Moesia Inferior
Classiana	Germania Inferior—Britain
Longiniana	
Patrui	ix. 733
Picentiana	Germania Superior
Pomponiani	Germania Inferior
Rusonis	Germania Superior
Sabiniana	Britain
Scaevae	x. 6011
Siliana C. R.	Africa—Pannonia

Cohorts

A.	I Gallica C. R. E.	Tarraconensis
	II Gallica	Tarraconensis
	I Gallorum	Aquitania
	I Gallorum Dacia	Dacia
	II Gallorum	Moesia Inferior
	II Gallorum Macedonica E.	Moesia Superior—Dacia
	II Gallorum	Mauretania Caesariensis
	II Gallorum E.	Britain
	III Gallorum	Germania Superior— Moesia Inferior
	III Gallorum	Spain
	IV Gallorum	Moesia Inferior
	IV Gallorum	Raetia
	IV Gallorum	Britain
	V Gallorum	Pannonia—Moesia Superior
	V Gallorum	Britain
	VI Gallorum	vi. 1449
	VII Gallorum	Moesia Inferior
	VIII, IX and X Gallorum supposed on account of the existence of	
	XI Gallorum	Dalmatia

AQUITANIA.

Alae.
None.

AQUITANIA (CONTINUED).

Cohorts

A. I Aquitanorum V. E.	Germania Superior
I Aquitanorum	Germania Superior—Britain
II Aquitanorum	Germania Superior—Raetia
III Aquitanorum E.C.R.	Germania Superior
IV Aquitanorum E. C. R.	Germania Superior
I Biturigum	Germania Superior
II Biturigum	xiii. 6812

NARBONENSIS.

Alae.

A. Augusta Vocontiorum	Germania Inferior—Britain
Vocontiorum	Egypt.

Cohorts.
None.

ALPES.   (All the little Alpine provinces.)

Alae.

A. Vallensium.	Germania Superior

Cohorts.

A. I Alpinorum	Pannonia Inferior
I Alpinorum E.	Pannonia Inferior
I Alpinorum E.	Dacia
I Alpinorum	Britain
II Alpinorum E.	Pannonia Superior
III Alpinorum E.	Dalmatia
I Ligurum	Alpes Maritimae—Germania Superior
II Gemina Ligurum et Corsorum	Sardinia
I Montanorum	Noricum—Pannonia—Dacia.
II Montanorum C. R.	Pannonia Inferior
I Montanorum	Palestine
Trumplinorum	v. 4910

RAETIA.

Alae.
None.

RAETIA (CONTINUED).

Cohorts.

A. I Helvetiorum	Germania Superior
I Raetorum	Raetia
I Raetorum E.	Cappadocia
II Raetorum C.R.	Germania Superior
II Raetorum	Raetia

Two cohorts III Raetorum supposed on account of the existence of

IV Raetorum E.	Cappadocia
IV Raetorum	Moesia Superior
V Raetorum	viii. 8934
VI Raetorum	Germania Superior
VII Raetorum	Germania Superior
VIII Raetorum C.R.	Pannonia—Dacia
Raetorum et Vindelicorum	Germania Superior
I Vindelicorum M.	Dacia

II and III Vindelicorum supposed on account of the existence of

IV Vindelicorum	Germania Superior
B. I Aelia Gaesatorum M.	Dacia

NORICUM

Alae.

A.	Noricorum	Germania Superior
	Cohorts.	
A.	I Noricorum	Pannonia Inferior

PANONNIA

Alae.
- A. I Pannoniorum   Africa
  - I Pannoniorum   Moesia Inferior
  - I Pannoniorum Tampiana   Britain
  - II Pannoniorum   Dacia
  - Pannoniorum   Pannonia Inferior
- B. I Illyricum   Dacia
  - Flavia Pannoniorum   Pannonia Inferior
  - Sarmatarum   Britain

PANNONIA (CONTINUED).

Cohorts

I Breucorum	Raetia
II Breucorum	Mauretania Caesariensis.
III Breucorum	ix. 4753.
IV Breucorum	Britain
V Breucorum	Noricum.
VI Breucorum	Moesia Superior.
VII Breucorum	Pannonia Inferior.
VIII Breucorum	xiii. 7801.
I Pannoniorum	Germania Superior—Britain.
I Pannoniorum	Mauretania Caesariensis.
I Augusta Pannoniorum	Egypt.
I Pannoniorum et Dalmatarum	χ. 5829.
II Pannoniorum	Britain
III Pannoniorum	Britain
IV Pannoniorum	iii. 12631, ix. 3924.
I Varcianorum supposed on account of the existence of	
II Varcianorum	Germania Inferior.
B. I Ulpia Pannoniorum M.E.	Pannonia Superior.

DALMATIA.

Alae.
None.
Cohorts.

A. I	Dalmatarum	Britain.
II	Dalmatarum	Britain.
III	Dalmatarum	Germania Superior.
IV	Dalmatarum	Germania Superior.
V	Dalmatarum	Germania Superior.
VI	Dalmatarum E.	Mauretania Caesariensis.
VII	Dalmatarum E.	Mauretania Caesariensis.
B. I	Dalmatarum M.	Dalmatia.
II	Dalmatarum M.	Dalmatia.
III	Dalmatarum M.E.C.R.	Dacia.
IV	Dalmatarum M.	iii. 1474.

MOESIA.

Alae.

A. Bosporanorum	Syria—Dacia.
B. I Vespasiana Dardanorum	Moesia Inferior.

Cohorts.

A. Bosporanorum M.	Cappadocia.
I Bosporiana	Pannonia Superior
II Bosporanorum	χ. 270.
B. I Aurelia Dardanorum	Moesia Superior.
II Aurelia Dardanorum M. E.	Moesia Superior.

DACIA.

Alae

B. I Ulpia Dacorum	Cappadocia.

Cohorts

B. I Ulpia Dacorum	Syria
I Aelia Dacorum M	Britain
II Augusta Dacorum	Pannonia.
Dacorum	Syria.
I Aurelia Dacorum supposed on account of the existence of	
II Aurelia Dacorum	Pannonia Superior.

THRACE

Alae.

A. Thracum Herculania	Syria
I Augusta Thracum	Raetia
I Thracum	Germania Inferior.—Britain.
I Thracum Mauretana	Egypt
I Thracum V. S.	Pannonia Inferior.
I Thracum Victrix	Pannonia Superior.
II Augusta Thracum	Mauretania Caesariensis.
III Augusta Thracum S.	Pannonia Superior.
III Thracum	Syria

Cohorts.

I Augusta Thracum E.	Pannonia Inferior.
I Thracum Germanica C. R. E.	Germania Superior—Pannonia
I Thracum M.	Palestine.
I Thracum S.	Dacia.
I Thracum E.	Pannonia Inferior.
I Thracum Syriaca	Palestine—Moesia Superior.

THRACE.

Cohorts (continued).

I Thracum	Germania Inferior—Britain.
II Augusta Thracum	Pannonia Inferior.
II Gemella Thracum	Africa.
II Thracum Syriaca	Syria.
II Thracum E.	Egypt.
II Thracum E.	Britain.
III Thracum V.	Raetia.
III Thracum C. R.	Raetia.
III Augusta Thracum E.	Syria.
III Thracum Syriaca	Syria.
IV Thracum Syriaca	Syria.
IV Thracum E.	Germania Superior.

```
        V  Thracum supposed on account of the existence of
        VI  Thracum                    Germania Superior—Britain—
                                        Pannonia—Dacia.
    B. I Flavia Bessorum                Macedonia.
       II Flavia Bessorum               Moesia Inferior.
```

MACEDONIA.

Alae.
None.

Cohorts.
```
A. Macedonum E.                    A. E. 1908. 58.
    I  Cyrrhesticorum supposed on account of the existence of
    II  Cyrrhesticorum             Dalmatia.
```

GALATIA.

Alae.
```
A. VII Phrygum                     Syria.
```
Cohorts.
```
B. I Ulpia Galatarum               Palestine.
   II Ulpia Galatarum              Palestine.
```

GALATIA.

Cohorts (continued).
```
III Ulpia Galatarum                Egypt.
I    Ulpia Paflagonum supposed on account of the existence of
II   Ulpia Paflagonum              Syria.
III  Ulpia Paflagonum              Syria.
```

CILICIA

Alae.
None.
Cohorts.
```
    A. I Cilicum                   Moesia Inferior.
       II Cilicum supposed on account of the existence of
       III  Cilicum                Egypt
    B. I Flavia Cilicum E.         Egypt.
```

CYPRUS.

Alae.
None.
Cohorts.
```
A. I, II, and III Cypria  supposed on account of the existence of
```

CRETE AND CYRENAICA.

Alae.

None.

Cohorts.

A. I Cretum	Moesia Superior.
I Cyrenaica	Germania Superior.
II Augusta Cyrenaica	Germania Superior.
III Cyrenaica S.	*A. E.* 1896. 10.
III Augusta Cyrenaica	*Römische Mitteilungen,* iii. 77.

SYRIA.

Alae.

A. Hamiorum	Mauretania Tingitana.
I Augusta Parthorum	Mauretania Caesariensis.
Parthorum V.	xiii. 10024
B. I Commagenorum	Egypt—Noricum.

Cohorts.

A. I Antiochensium	Moesia Superior.
I Apamenorum S. E.	Egypt
I Chalcidenorum E.	Africa
II Chalcidenorum	Moesia Inferior.
III and IV Chalcidenorum supposed on account of the existence of	
V Chalcidenorum	Syria.
I Damascenorum	Palestine.
I Hamiorum	Britain.
II Hamiorum	viii. 10654.
I Hemesenorum M.S.E.CR.	Pannonia Inferior.
I Sagittariorum	Germania Superior—Dacia (?).
II Sagittariorum supposed on account of the existence of	
III Sagittariorum	iii. 335, xiv. 3935.
I Tyriorum	Moesia Inferior.
B. I Flavia Canathenorum M.	Raetia.
I Flavia Chalcidenorum S. E.	Syria.
I Flavia Commagenorum Dacia	
II Flavia Commagenorum	Dacia
III, IV, and V Commagenorum supposed on account of the existence of	
VI Commagenorum	Africa
I Flavia Damascenorum M. E.	Germania Superior.
I Ulpia Sagittariorum E.	Syria.
I Aelia Sagittariorum M.E.	Pannonia Superior.
I Nova Surorum M. S.	Pannonia Inferior.

PALESTINE.

A. I Augusta Ituraeorum	Pannonia Inferior.
Sebastenorum	Palestine—Mauretania Caesariensis.

Cohorts.

A. I Ascalonitanorum Felix E.	Syria.
I Augusta Ituraeorum S.	Pannonia—Dacia.
I Ituraeorum	Germania Superior—Dacia.

II Ituraeorum E.	Egypt.
III Ituraeorum	Egypt.
IV, V, and VI Ituraeorum supposed on account of the existence of VII Ituraeorum	Egypt.
I Sebastenorum M.	Palestine.

ARABIA.

Alae.

A. I Ulpia Dromedariorum M.	Syria.

Cohorts.

B. I Ulpia Petraeorum M. E.		Syria.
II Ulpia Petraeorum M.E.		xi. 5669.
III Ulpia Petraeorum M. E.		Cappadocia.
IV Ulpia Petraeorum		Palestine.
V Ulpia Petraeorum E.	Syria.	
VI Ulpia Petraeorum		Palestine.

EGYPT.

Alae.

None.

Cohorts.

A. I Thebaeorum E.		Egypt.
II Thebaeorum	Egypt.	

AFRICA

Alae.

A. Afrorum	Germania Inferior.
Gaetulorum V.	Palestine.
B. I Ulpia Afrorum supposed on account of the existence of	
II Ulpia Afrorum	Egypt.
I Flavia Gaetulorum	Moesia Inferior.

Cohorts.

A. I Afrorum C. R. E.	x. 5841.
I Cirtensium supposed on account of the existence of	
II Cirtensium	Mauretania Caesariensis.
I Cisipadensium	Moesia Superior.
I Gaetulorum	viii. 7039.
B. I Flavia Afrorum supposed on account of the existence of	
II Flavia Afrorum	Africa.
I Ulpia Afrorum E.	Egypt.
I Flavia Musulamiorum	Mauretania Caesariensis.
I Flavia Numidarum	Lycia.
II Flavia Numidarum	Dacia.

MAURETANIA.

Alae.

None.

Cohorts

A.	Maurorum M.	Africa.
	Maurorum M.	Pannonia Inferior.
	Maurorum Quingenaria	Pannonia Inferior.

TARRACONENSIS.

Alae.

A. I Arvacorum	Pannonia Superior.
II Arvacorum	Moesia Inferior.
I Asturum	Britain.
I Asturum	Moesia Inferior.

TARRACONENSIS. ALAE (CONTINUED).

II Asturum	Britain
III Asturum	xi. 3007.
I Hispanorum Campagonum	Dacia.
I Hispanorum	Germania Superior—Dacia
I Hispanorum Auriana	Noricum.
I Lemavorum	Tarraconensis.
I Hispanorum Vettonum C. R.	Britain.
B. II Flavia Hispanorum	Spain.

Cohorts.

A. I	Asturum		Germania Superior—Britain.
I	Asturum		Noricum.
II	Asturum		Germania Inferior—Britain.
III	Asturum		Mauretania Tingitana.
IV	Asturum supposed on account of the existence of		
V	Asturum		Germania Inferior.
VI	Asturum		ii. 2637.
I	Asturum et Callaecorum		Mauretania Tingitana.
II	Asturum et Callaecorum		Pannonia Inferior.
I	Ausetanorum		ii. 1181.
I	Bracaraugustanorum		Moesia Inferior
II	Bracaraugustanorum		vi. 1838.
III	Bracaraugustanorum	Britain.	
III	Bracaraugustanorum	Raetia.	
III	Bracaraugustanorum	Palestine.	
IV	Bracaraugustanorum	Palestine.	
V	Bracaraugustanorum	Raetia.	
I	Cantabrorum supposed on account of the existence of		
II	Cantabrorum		Palestine.
	Carietum et Veniaesum		v. 4373.
I	Celtiberorum		Spain.
I	Celtiberorum		Britain.
II	Celtiberorum supposed on account of the existence of		
III	Celtiberorum		Spain.
I	Hispanorum		Dacia.

TARRACONENSIS. COHORTS (CONTINUED).

Hispanorum V. E.	Moesia Inferior.

I Hispanorum E.	Britain.
I Hispanorum E.	Egypt.
II Hispanorum	Germania Superior.
II Hispanorum Scutata Cyrenaica	Dacia.
II Hispanorum E.	Africa.
II Hispanorum E.	Cappadocia.
III Hispanorum	Germania Superior.
IV Hispanorum	Dacia.
V Hispanorum	Germania Superior—Moesia Superior, xi. 4376.
VI Hispanorum	Dalmatia—Syria.
I Lucensium E.	Germania Inferior.
I Lucensium Hispanorum	Moesia Inferior.
II Lucensium	Spain.
III Lucensium	Syria.
IV Lucensium	Pannonia Superior.
V Lucensium et Callaecorum	Britain.
I Fida Vardullorum M. E. C. R.	
Vasconum supposed on account of the existence of	
II Hispanorum Vasconum C. R. E.	Britain.
B. I Flavia Hispanorum	Mauretania Caesariensis.
I Flavia Hispanorum M. E.	Moesia Superior.
Flavia Ulpianorum M. E. C. R.	Dacia.
I Aelia Hispanorum M. E.	Britain.

LUSITANIA.

Alae.

None.

Cohorts.

A. I Augusta Praetoria Lusitanorum E.	Egypt.
I Lusitanorum	Pannonia Inferior.
I Lusitanorum Cyrenaica	Moesia Inferior.
II Lusitanorum E.	Egypt.

LUSITANIA. COHORTS (CONTINUED).

III	Lusitanorum E.	Germania Inferior—Pannonia Inferior.
IV and V	Lusitanorum supposed on account of the existence of	
VI	Lusitanorum	Raetia.
VII	Lusitanorum E.	Africa—Raetia.

ALAE. SARDINIA AND CORSICA.

None.

Cohorts.

A. I Corsorum C. R.	Mauretania Caesariensis.
I Corsorum	Sardinia.
I Sardorum	Sardinia.

II Sardorum E.	Mauretania Caesariensis.
B. I Gemina Sardorum et Corsorum	Sardinia.
II Gemina Ligurum et Corsorum	Sardinia.

These last two regiments seem to have been formed by amalgamating the cohorts I Corsorum, I Sardorum, and I Ligurum, which appear in Sardinia in the pre-Flavian period, but not later.

COHORTES VOLUNTARIORUM AND OTHER REGIMENTS OF ROMAN CITIZENS.

The character of these regiments has already been discussed on pp. 65-7, where the origin of the greater number, at any rate, was traced to the exceptional levies made during the Pannonian revolt of 6-9, and after the defeat of Varus in the latter year. This levy included not only free-born Roman citizens, *ingenui*, but also freedmen enrolled in *cohortes voluntariorum*. The latter form a series numbered up to thirty-two, which may have included the *cohortes ingenuorum*. The latter may, however, have been numbered separately, and it must be admitted that the presence of a Cohors IV Voluntariorum is rather against the hypothesis, previously advanced, that the first six numbers of the series were reserved for the *ingenui*. It is impossible to argue from the fact that a *cohors voluntariorum* and a *cohors ingenuorum* never appear bearing the same numbers, since the series has many gaps, and only the following regiments can be traced:

I Ingenuorum C. R.	v. 3936.
IV Voluntariorum C. R.	Pannonia Superior.
VI Ingenuorum C. R.	Germania Inferior.
VIII Voluntariorum C. R.	Dalmatia.
XIII Voluntariorum C. R.	iii. 6321.
XV Voluntariorum C. R.	Germania Inferior.
XVIII Voluntariorum C. R.	Pannonia Superior.
XIX Voluntariorum C. R.	vii. 383.
XXIII Voluntariorum C. R.	Pannonia Superior.
XXIV Voluntariorum C. R.	Germania Superior.
XXVI Voluntariorum CR.	Germania Superior.
XXX Voluntariorum C. R.	Germania Superior.
XXXII Voluntariorum C. R.	Germania Superior.

The following regiments seem to have a similar character, although we know nothing concerning the occasion of their creation:

I. Italica Voluntariorum C. R.	xiv. 171.
II. Italica Voluntariorum C. R. M.	Cappadocia.
I Campanorum Voluntariorum C. R.	Dalmatia—Pannonia Inferior.

Lastly, a series of at least seven regiments bearing the inexplicable title of Campestris, of which only the following have left traces:

III Campestris	Dacia.
VII Campestris	Syria.

The following three regiments should perhaps be included in the same category:

Ala I C. R.	Pannonia Inferior.
Cohors Apuleia C. R.	Cappadocia.
Cohors I Lepidiana C. R.	Moesia Inferior.

In a final section I have grouped together regiments which bear non-ethnical titles, and a few cases of ethnical titles which are at present inexplicable, owing to our ignorance of the situation of the tribes referred to. In the former case it must, however, be remembered that many of these regiments may have had ethnical titles which are not mentioned in the only references to them which we possess.

Alae.

Augusta Noricum.

Augusta	Moesia Inferior.
Augusta	Egypt.
Augusta C. R.	Pannonia Inferior.
Augusta Germanica	Pisidia.
Augusta Moesica	Germania Inferior.
Augusta Syriaca	Syria.
Augusta ob virtutem appellata	Britain.
Claudia Nova	Dalmatia—Germania Superior —Moesia Inferior.
I Augusta Gemina Colonorum Constantium	Cappadocia. *A. E.* 1911. 107.
I Ulpia Contariorum M.C.R.	Pannonia Superior.
Flavia	Africa.
I Flavia Fidelis M. Raetia.	
I Flavia Gemelliana	Raetia.
I Flavia Gemina	Germania Superior.
I Flavia Singularium C. R.	Raetia.
II Flavia M.	Raetia.
Miliaria	Mauretania Caesariensis.
Miliaria	Dacia.
I Augusta Nerviana M.	Mauretania Caesariensis.
I Praetoria C. R.	Syria.
Scubulorum	Germania Superior.
I Ulpia Singularium	Syria.
Tautorum	Victrix Tarraconensis.
II Ulpia Auriana	Cappadocia.

Cohorts.

Aelia Expedita	viii. 9358.
I Augusta	Syria.
II Augusta supposed on account of the existence of	
III Augusta	vi. 3508.
Baetica	v. 5127.
I Classica	Germania Inferior.
I Aelia Classica	Britain.
II Classica	Syria.
Claudia E.	Cappadocia.
III Coll ...	Moesia Inferior.
I Dongonum supposed on account of the existence of	
II Dongonum	Britain.

The Lollianus inscription (iii. 600) mentions a mysteriously named Cohors II Equitum, which seems also to be referred to on an Italian inscription (v. 2841) as Cohors II Equitatum. The Cohors VI Equestris mentioned by Pliny *(Ep. ad Tra.* 106) may belong to the same series. The best explanation of these curious titles is to suppose that they are all varieties of *equitata.*

I Flavia E.	Africa.
I Flavia E.	Germania Inferior.
Flaviana	*C. I. G.* 3615.
V Gemina	Palestine.
I Latabiensium	Germania Inferior.
Maritima	ii. 2224.
Miliaria	Syria.
Naut ...	Alpes Maritimae.
I Augusta Nerviana Velox	Mauretania Caesariensis.
I Nurritanorum	Mauretania Caesariensis.
Scutata C . R .	Egypt.
I Aelia Singularium	Mauretania Caesariensis.
I Ulpia supposed on account of the existence of	
II Ulpia E. C. R. Syria.	

This last section completes our survey of the auxiliary forces of the Empire so far as they are known to us, and it is some satisfaction to feel that so far as the mere names of the regiments go our knowledge is now approaching completion. The recently discovered diploma for Moesia Superior $(A. E.$ 1912. 128), which gave the names of twenty-four regiments which were stationed in the province in 103, did not mention one previously unknown to us, and a glance at the *Année Épigraphique* for the past ten years will show how rarely a fresh name appears among the numerous inscriptions dealing with the auxilia. This knowledge does not, of course, carry us very far; while so many regiments are merely known to us by name from one or two casual inscriptions, we can tell neither the total number of auxilia maintained at any one time nor the relative strength of the frontier garrisons, and a host of minor problems are even further from solution. The very fact, however, that new evidence is now so slow to accumulate seemed to justify the attempt to utilize the available material and state summarily such conclusions as are at present attainable on a subject of some interest and importance to all students of the Roman Empire.